KENN BROOKS:

MY LIFE AND TIMES:

VOLUME 2

AF059785

by

KENN BROOKS

DEDICATION

I dedicate this book to my Daughter Annette Brooks Trujillo for all the proof reading and suggestions, getting me onto and out of the computer, coming to my aid when my big fingers hit some wayward keys making a big problem to be fixed.

Kenn Brooks' life story continues in Volume 2 with post-high school experiences as he strives to juggle work, college, and marital life simultaneously.

This is a continuation of the story of the man who was not afraid to take on any task or endeavor leading to a higher quality of life for himself and those around him. Kenn tackled various employment opportunities to enhance his life experience to the extent that his peers regarded him as a well-rounded individual. He was often sought after for advice regarding outdoor-oriented tasks and assistance in helping other individuals to complete projects that were familiar to him through life experience. His ingenuity and ability to problem solve were highly regarded by those who worked with him daily. Above all, Kenn Brooks demonstrated kindness and empathy in a world seemingly caught up with personal gain rather than altruistic motives.

Written by Timothy J. O'Leary, III, Author

The following photo was unfortunately omitted from the first volume entitled Kenn Brooks: My Life, Volume 1, Page 118.

Ralph L. Sturgis

otherwise known to the rest of us as **GRAMP** or **GRAMPIE**.

He was a hard working man, but always had time for his family or even a perfect stranger. Whether it was a wink, a wave or just to tease, which he liked to do the best.

His life was Grammie and family and most of all his horses. He could talk forever when it came to them. When he saw a good looking horse a twinkle would come over his eyes that most people couldn't understand.

People would come from miles to see Gramp and Grammie with their horses. I never saw such a strong man in my life. On a 90 degree day most men would want to sit and relax, but not Gramp. I can still see him driving that old hay wagon with sweat running down the sides of his face, and at every horn he would raise his hard calloused hand with a friendly wave.

I am proud to be a Sturgis because I know I can do anything. Gramp told me so, and Sturgis' are a strong breed, and in his life he proved it. I'll miss the noises he made when he talked to the horses, and watching him take those long strides across the yard. But most of all I'll miss him.

I love you always Gramp. But I know you're there like the old stone wall that surrounds the fields. I will always stop and listen for your words.

Love, Audra

I still see you sitting in the shed door catching some sun. You are missed deeply by all!

Love you always,
Your sons, daughters, daughters-in-law, sons-in-law, grandchildren, great and great-great

MR. AND MRS. CHARLES HUFF

They lived on the Old Standish Road on the back side of Bonny Eagle Pond. Son Bryce and Daughter Alicia were in Mrs. Twombley's 4-H Club. Charles was the Personnel Director for the Maine Medical Center. Willine Twombley made arrangements for Tim and me to ride with him to Portland and back in the fall of 1961.

Either Willine or my mother Lillian would drop us boys off at his house at the end of his road. Mr. Huff drive a VW Beetle which did not have any heat. We had to wear heavy boots to keep our feet warm and carried our shoes. Tim was dropped off at the U.S.M. Campus on the way in. I would walk to and from the hospital to the college on Danforth Street. On the way home Mr. Huff and I would stop at the college lobby to pick up Tim. I was already in the front seat, and I let him have it on the way in.

The new Plummers Store was not built until 1969, or that would have made a good place to meet Mr. Huff.

Northeaster Business College,
97 Danforth Street, Portland, Maine.
Owners: Earl Grand and Miss Heath.

The owners formed this College to help Veterans using the G.I. Bill.

Courses and Instructors

Law	Earl Grant
Accounting	Myron Libby
English	Miss Heath
Typing	Mrs. Sullivan
Office Machines	Phil Tanerillo

Classmates

Duane Decker	Janet Gorman
Waldo Harwood	Roland Huribise

John Lord

Larry Merrill

Donald Meserve   Edwaard Norton

James Ryan

Wallis Burk

Gordon Huribise

Clifford Thomas

> The last three students were those that I tutored.

Mr. Myron Libby's philosophy for life:

First: "Find value in things that have been forgotten or tossed away."

Second: "You got to get out of the truck if you want to make any money. You have got to show up, engage, and work hard to make a difference."

Third: "Love hard, love wholeheartedly, never give up, and provide for your family."

What I got to know about some of my classmates.

James Ryan (Jimmy) lived in North Deering and worked at Rudy's Market on Washington Avenue by the I-95 overpass. He would meet his future wife Dorothy while she shopped with her mother. When they came into the store, Jimmy would make every effort to be in proximity to her. Jimmy got me playing ping pong on our lunch breaks. We got really good at it and sometimes played doubles with some of the others. Jimmy was the life of the party and kept the study group laughing at his jokes.

Larry Merrill was from South Paris. He had found a small apartment with an elderly lady in her home at the corner of Danforth and St. John Streets. He also did maintenance work for part of this rent. I always had a good time when I visited with his dad and mom and brother Dale.

Mrs. Merrill ran an elderly boarding house having two or three people at a time in her home. We became good friends He was the Best Man at my wedding.

John Lord was from Casco and his parents' raised chickens which were sold for meat. They wanted John to learn accounting to help them with the farm books. Unfortunately, his dad became ill, and they had to go out of business.
John had a nice new car and a heavy foot. He got Jimmy and me to go for a ride. He took us up High Street, left onto Congress Street going a little too fast. When we got down to St. John Street, he stopped at the light, made another left, and laid rubber and, stopped real quick. He scared us all so bad! We got back to the college and never went in his car again. Others soon learned the same lesson.
Duane Decker was from Sebago. Duane and his dad worked for Maine Hardware

on Congress Street. He showed us a little restaurant on Spring Street where you could get a good quick lunch fairly priced.

LARRY MERRILL

Duane Decker, 74

WESTBROOK - Duane Decker, 74, of Mayflower Road, died unexpectedly on Monday, September 18, 2017, at Mercy Hospital.

Born in Sebago, Duane was the son of the late Lindley and Eleanor (Cushman) Decker. He graduated from Potter Academy in 1961.

Following school, Duane was drafted by the United States Army, where he served in France during the Vietnam War. Following his honorable discharge, Duane returned home to Maine, where he worked as an operations manager for Maine Hardware and later Bodien and Johnson and B.W. Webb, all jobs he enjoyed for over 40 years.

Duane married Elaine MacLean on Sept. 14, 1996. Together, they shared 21 years of marriage full of laughter and love.

Duane was always known to be doing something. Whether it was puttering in his garage, restoring old furniture or even something as simple as changing a light in a closet, Duane always had a project.

In addition, he enjoyed watching boxing, especially the fighters at the Portland Boxing Club. His family remembers how he was always interested in going to matches at the Expo, and closely followed local boxers.

Above all else, Duane will forever be remembered for his love of togetherness. He enjoyed being surrounded by his family and friends, especially at his famous lobster bakes and barbecues. He had a wonderful sense of humor and could always make people laugh.

He is survived by his beloved wife, Elaine Decker, of Westbrook; children, Kathy Globbi and husband Mike, of Portland; Stephanie Skelton and husband Tom, of Standish; Michael Leahy and wife Ann Marie, of Haverhill, Mass.; Tom Leahy and wife Pam, of Portland; and Anthony Decker and wife Kathy, of Westbrook; daughter-in-law, Elizabeth Decker, of Westbrook; and grandchildren, Nicholas, Andrew, Matthew, Michael, Ryan, Erin, Katelyn, Jonathan and Christopher. He is also survived by his great-grandchildren; sisters, Leanne Reinhard and Ixetland Brian, of Naples; and Linda Gadbois and husband Norman, of Sebago; aunt, Lorraine Barrault, of Westbrook; and several nieces and nephews.

Visiting hours will be held Saturday, Sept. 23, from 11 a.m.- noon at the **Conroy-Tully Walker South Portland Chapel**, 1024 Broadway, South Portland. Duane's Celebration of Life will be held at noon, followed by a reception in the funeral home. To view Duane's memorial page or to share an online condolence, please visit www.ConroyTullyWalker.com

In lieu of flowers, memorial contributions may be made to the *Carin MacLean Foundation*: www.CarinMacLeanFoundation.com, or *Portland Boxing Club*, at: www.portlandboxingclub.org/donate

James Joseph Ryan
1942 - 2021

SCARBOROUGH – James Joseph Ryan, 79, passed away at home on Monday, Oct. 11, 2021, after complications from illness. He was born Sept. 2, 1942, in Portland, the son of Frederick J. and Margaret A. (Olmstead) Ryan.

Jim graduated from Portland High School Class of 1961. Following graduation, he went on to earn an associate degree in business from Northeastern Business School. While attending college and working as a clerk at Rudy's Market, he met Dorothy Bryant of Portland. He went on to marry his loving wife, Dotty, and they moved to Biddeford and eventually settled in Saco. He went to work at the WestPoint Pepperell mill in Biddeford for 12 years where he was a supervisor. When the mill closed, he went to work as a dispatcher with St. Johnsbury trucking. He was there for nearly 20 years until their operation shut down. He then worked for the Portland School Department as a custodian for 13 years, until he retired at age 67.

Jim and Dotty had two children together and in 1976, they took in his Jim's younger brother Tim due to their parents passing away. Tim was just transitioning to high school. As a family they enjoyed camping in the NH mountains, going to car races at Beech Ridge, Oxford, and Louden speedways. They also enjoyed going to see the Maine Mariners play hockey. They eventually moved to So. Portland and bought land in Orisfield for a camp. With the help of Jim's father, they built the camp which is still in the family today. After their children were grown, Jim and Dotty moved to their current residence in Scarborough. Through his adult life and into retirement Jim enjoyed listening to country music, watching Nascar & WWE wrestling on TV, eating KFC and socializing at both the Eagles Club in Portland, where he was a Golden Eagle and at the Moose Lodge in Scarborough. Jim and Dotty celebrated 50 years of marriage this year.

In addition to his parents, he was predeceased by two brothers, Barry & George Ryan. Surviving in addition to his wife Dorothy, are his sons John P. Ryan of Eustis, FL and Peter J. Ryan of So. Portland, ME; two grandchildren, Chelsie Ryan of Orlando, FL and Zachary Ryan of Limington, ME and their respective mothers, Melissa Doughty and Christine Amato who remain close to the family, as well as his younger brother Timothy J. Ryan and many nieces and nephews.

A service will be held at 11 a.m. on Wednesday, October 20 at Scarborough Free Baptist Church, 62 Mussey Road, Scarborough. A reception and light lunch will take place immediately afterwards at the church. Flowers can be sent to the church to arrive between 1 and 5 p.m. on Tuesday, Oct. 19. Deliveries will be accepted at the rear door. Condolences can be mailed to Dotty Ryan at 7 Skyline Street, Scarborough, ME 04074.

John and Peter Ryan want to express that they loved their father very much. Tim Ryan wants to express his appreciation of his brother's strength. He will be missed.

The family would like to thank all of those who have been there to help whenever it was needed, including hospice and hospital staff, friends, neighbors, family, and the congregation.

Jim will be buried at Brooklawn Memorial Park, 2002 Congress Street, Portland, at a future date.

To share memories of Jim or to leave the family an online condolence, please visit www.coastalcremationservices.com.

Those who wish to make gifts in remembrance of Jim may do so to either So. Maine Hospice,
890 US Route 1, Scarborough, ME 04074
or to the
Scarborough Free Baptist Church.

§ Coastal
Cremation Services

Roland W. Hurtubise
1943 - 2020

STANDISH - Roland W. Hurtubise, 76, passed away after a long illness, on June 12, 2020. He was born on Feb. 14, 1943.

He is survived by his two sons, Todd and Brian Hurtubise; and his two grandchildren, Jordyn "Grasshopper" Hurtubise and Colby Hurtubise. He will be lonely without his "Shadow," a chocolate lab whom he found great companionship in and were always together.

Roland is best known for the restaurant he owned and ran with his family, "The INLET" for 36 years. He was a Past Master at the former Standish Masonic Lodge.

Per his request there will be no viewing or service.

Online condolence messages can be submitted at the **Chad E. Poitras Cremation and Funeral Service** website, www.mainefuneral.com

Janet Gorman and *Donald Meserve* were from Portland. *Edward Norton* was from South Portland. *Roland* and *Gordon Huribise* were from Yarmouth. *Waldo Harwood* was from Old Orchard Beach. *Clifford Thomas* was from Buxton, and *Wallis Burk* was from Cape Elizabeth.

Kenneth Brooks, Kenn as I wished to be called, was from Standish by the Saco River and Bonny Eagle Pond.

MY NEW HAMPSHIRE DATE

My Brother Ralph had spent some summer days helping our Grandfather Brooks on the farm. Carol and Verna Libby, friends of Grandpa's and Grandma's, stopped for a visit on their way home from the village store. They had their two daughters with them, Brenda and Barbara. Ralph and Ralph III were asked to go up to their farm to help with something.

A couple of weekends later, Ralph had me take him up there for a visit. We found out that Barbara was not allowed to go out on dates. I got a date with Brenda to go to the Drive-In Theater in North Conway. Ralph said that he would stay and play games with Barbara. That is what we did the next weekend.

When Brenda and I got to the Drive-In, they were playing Walt Disney children's movies that we had seen years before. We then drove around and she showed me the area before getting something to eat. We sat and talked about school, living in the country versus city life, etc. I got her home a little early. We did not really hit it off. (See photo of Brenda Libby on following page.)

THE TRIP TO SITE IN GUNS – FALL OF 1961

We had made plans to skip school and go to Ryan's camp in Otisfield to do some shooting and site in our guns. I got permission from Mr. huff to let me bring my 30-30 rifle with me.

Then I walked from the Maine Medical Center down Congress Street to a parking lot of Porteous, Mitchell and Braun. Larry worked part-time there for a while, long enough to meet his future wife, Patricia. Try walking a Portland Street today with a gun and you might not get too far.
Next, Larry drove us out to Jim Ryan's house where we met John Lord. Thank God his car was too small for the four of us with guns and ammo, so we used Jim's Dad's station wagon.
We had an early wet snow in October making for slushy roads. Going up Route 100 to Gray, we slid off into a marsh and bent the right front rim. We had just

passed a Merrill Transport gas tanker and just got out of his way in time.

We had to be towed to the nearest garage to get a new rim and have it installed. While it was being fixed, a State Trooper came in for a repair. We were worried he would see, or find out we had the guns, but his light was quickly fixed, and he left. When the car was done and the bill split among us, we went back to Jim's. We then all went home and never tried to do it again.

DEERING OAKS PARK – SPRING OF 1962

One nice spring day, I had to study for a test in Business Law and decided to do it in my car in Deering Oaks. I had been there reading for a while when, all of a sudden, this guy was at the passenger side door and wanting to get in. I lifted my empty revolver and pointed it at him. He backed up quickly and his eyes went wide in surprise and I think he shit himself before he ran. His legs could not take him quickly enough across Park Avenue.

I do not remember why I even had the gun in the car that day.

1962 MY THIRD SUMMER AT S.D. WARREN Another summer of mostly painting. But one time they needed more help on the roof of the building next to the smokestack. I was assigned to move things around. One day while the others went to lunch, I ate out of my brown bag. Then with time on my hands, I decided to climb the smokestack ladder for a view.

PHOTO OF MY SISTER CAROL (16) ON THE FRONT PORCH OF THE HOUSE IN 1962

I had been on many ladders and knew that if you go up you must come down. I also know that you do not do any sight-seeing while climbing. Now with the height of the building and some twenty rounds on the ladder, the view was something else. All of the cities of Westbrook, Portland, South Portland, Cape Elizabeth came into view. About twenty miles out to sea I could see a ship come into view. It was just beautiful. A deep breath and my eyes back on the ladder, I retreated undetected.

COLLEGE YEAR TWO – FALL OF 1962

Timothy Twombly had a blue scooter, and I had a very old Pontiac for our commute. Donald Meserve and Jimmy Ryan, both Portland natives, introduced the rest of us to a bowling alley which was downstairs in the cellar in the building at the corner of High and Free Streets. I cannot remember what was in the building upstairs, but it is next door to the Portland Museum of Art and across from Hay's Drug Store. A lot of our free time was spent there.

Larry Merrill was working nights at the Lafayette Hotel, which was built in 1903, as a night clerk.

  A strange call from one of the guests who said there was a pounding on the wall in the next room. They could not get the older lady on the phone. Next, they went up and let themselves in with a master key. She had slipped in the shower and fell wedging her boob between the faucet and the wall, no further description needed. I was working at the college for my tuition. We were a few weeks into my second year when Mr. Libby came to me to ask me to help with three students coming into the class behind me. He wanted me to help them catch up with the rest of the class by helping them in the afternoon after class.

Clifford Thomas was from Buxton and Wallis Burk, a service veteran was from Cape Elizabeth. Wallis was the oldest student at the time by about 15 years and he was the biggest person and drove a small Volkswagen Beetle. He was a quick learner and he helped some of his classmates.

Don Baker ran Wass Garage which he had taken over after years of working for "Good Old Dad", his father-in-law.

I met Don through my college friend Larry Merrill when my car broke down at college. Don had been recommended to Larry by someone at the hotel. Don was a very good mechanic, always looking out for his customers in the downtown Portland area and he was a blessing to the college drivers.

John Lord finished the second year and took a job at King Cole Foods in South Portland.

Duane Decker worked part time at Maine Hardware Company upon finishing the second year of college. He was promoted at Maine Hardware Company and stayed there his whole career. He helped Maine Hardware Company make the move to their new store at Union Station Plaza on St. John Street.

TOP OF THE EAST

After bowling one Friday night, myself, Don Meserve, Ed Norton, Jim Ryan, John Lord, and Larry Merrill decided to check out the "Top of the East", a bar and restaurant at the top of the Eastland Hotel in Portland. They ordered their drinks and I ordered milk. We were enjoying the view when they brought our drinks. They wanted $2.50 for a $0.50 glass of milk. Now you know that did not set well with this farm boy. I let them know at the top of my voice. "You want $2.50 for a $0.50 glass of milk?" All customers at their tables looked up. "I brought this group up here and we can all leave now."

"No, no, I'll give it to you free." "Thank you, we'll stay and enjoy the view."

I left $0.50 on the counter. Maybe I helped start the concession for designated drivers.

THE PARKING LOT JOB

Larry Merrill was working at the Lafayette Hotel when he heard about the owner of the parking lot at 136 Park Street was looking for help. He wanted someone to work from 3 to 6 and close the lot for the night. I went up and got the job. I had to have cars ready to go for the monthly customers; sometimes you had to move cars around as some were double parked. In the winter I had to clean off the snow and I had the cars warmed up when they got out of work. This fit right in after my college janitor job.

One day at college, Larry told me, "A well-to-do gentleman, a regular at the hotel, was coming in and I should be around as he liked to give away $20.00 bills." The staff called him Mr. Goldbrick, not his real name, and always said it out of his hearing.

A regular monthly customer at the parking lot, Fritze Coyne who worked for a TV station was usually the last one to leave. A very pretty and well-dressed lady was the only one to give me a x-mass gift, a nice tie.

MY LIMITED MOUNTAIN SKIING

David McNutt and I were skiing at Pleasant Mountain (now Shawnee Peak). It was my first time. I was wearing woolen clothes on a very sunny day which made for sticky snow. I fell a lot and I looked like a snowman.

My ski poles were very old bamboo ones, so I rented a pair for the day. I was coming down too fast, sliding to my left towards a steep drop off, I planted the left ski pole and slid up against it hard, causing it to bend at a right angle.

When I took them back, he said, "I think you have bought them." I took them home and repaired the broken one. I still have them. One of the next times down, when I fell, my ski binding came undone, and I had to go into the woods for the ski. I had to use the restroom. Dave went for another run on a different and difficult trail that I did not think I could safely use. When I came out into the lobby, I saw a runaway ski coming right for the lodge as a dog was walking by. The ski went right through his body and hit the foundation of the building and the dog died. There was such a commotion with nothing that I could do. I went for another run before meeting up with Dave and going home.

RESIDENT
HUNTING LICENSE 1962   N⁰ 126163
STATE OF MAINE
Name: Violet McKay
174 Spring St   WESTBROOK
Age 59   Weight 132   Height 5'5"   Complexion med
Place Westbrook
Date Issued 10-26

Fee $2.25   Expires December 31, 1962

N⁰ 126163

STATE OF MAINE

Name: Violet McKay
Residence 174 Spring St Westbrook Me
Phone 245-3855

NILA MOULTON BROOKS, DAVID McNUTT, VIOLET McKAY'S RESIDENT HUNTING LICENSE

At college I made a date to take Elizabeth Edwards to Sunday River skiing. On Saturday morning I went to gas up the old black Buick at Plummers Store in West Buxton on my way to pick her up in South Portland. The car would not start after I filled the gas tank. It had to be towed to the car doctors. I never did get another date with her.

I went skiing only a very few times before getting married. I never had the money to buy new equipment. So, that was the end of my skiing days.

HOW I MET NILA IN DECEMBER 1962

David McNutt was a year behind me in high school and his sister Judy was a year ahead of me. I got to know David through our Key Club activities in my Junior and

Senior years. This gave me two years of Key Club conventions in Boston At that time, I was finishing my second year of college and Dave was in his first year at S.M.V.T.I., a vocational school in South Portland.

David had a cousin, Beverly Young, who lived in Buxton. On December 5, 1962, he stopped in to see her on his way from college by detouring to Buxton as it was not his direct way home. During his visit, he found out that a Buxton family had been burnt out and the community was having a benefit supper and dance for a fund raiser for them. Beverly told him that the neighborhood girls were asked to help serve supper. Their reward was free admission to the dance. She asked him to come and to find some other boys to come and she would introduce everyone. So, Dave proceeded up the road to stop and see me. "What are you doing tomorrow night?" he said. I said, "I don't know what we are going to do." Then he told me about the benefit at the Buxton Grange Hall and the invitation.

David and I could not get there early enough for the supper, but we made the dance. Beverly and Nila were sleep over buddies and were dropped off at the dance together. When we got there, we met them and several other gals. We headed up to the dance hall while all the girls' cleared tables and finished the dishes. Nila and some others came up from downstairs and they had taken seats over in one corner and she watched me most of the evening.

When you square dance, you dance with everyone not just your partner. I had gone downstairs to use the restroom. Coming back up the stairs I heard them announce the last square dance, most had already selected a partner. So, I went down the line over in the corner – four no's', before Nila's yes. I thought she looked about sixteen, no matter it got me on the dance floor. The next dance was a waltz and I asked her if she would like to continue dancing. As we danced and talked a bit, I found out she was nineteen and only working part- time. She was impressed that I was in college and told me that, due to a medical operation on her sinusitis inflammation, she had not been able to start Bible College in Pennsylvania. Three more dances finished the evening program. Dave and I took Bev and Nila home. Xmas vacation week was coming up and we made a date to teach the girls to ski on Saturday. Their interest was somewhat lacking, and they failed at their attempts at staying upright. So, they had us inside playing board games. Nila and I made a date to go to the movies in

Portland and the dates continued. Even though Nila only lived a couple of miles away, and I about eight miles away, neither of us had been to the Grange Hall dances before.

Nila's sister Irene Starbird had a miscarriage and needed blood, so I gave blood and I have been giving blood ever since. I was really accepted by her family. Dad, Lesley, Mom, Francis, and siblings Lesley, Jr. (Sonny), Irene, Betty Ann, Kenneth, Nancy, and Janice.

RINGS

February 1963 after many more dates Nila and I swapped our 1961 class rings as a sign of going steady. Her Buxton ring and my Standish ring.

BRINKS SECURITY JOB – DON BAKER AT WASS GARAGE

Don Baker was the owner of Wass Garage. Wass Garage was located on the ground floor of a four-story building which had a parking area inside for offstreet parking. One of Don's customers using this service was a driver for Brinks (the Money people). He would keep his station wagon inside each night after his run. You used your own car and were paid expenses. Don did the maintenance on the station wagon. The job was taking canceled checks and papers, no cash, to Boston at the regional banks clearing house. You left Portland around 9 P.M., when you got there, you drove into a locked garage for the drop off. Then picked up the return paperwork about 1:00 A.M. And came back. In March of 1963, the Brinks driver was going to retire. Brinks offered the job to their day-time drivers, but none had come forward.

So, I applied for the job, but before I could get all the way through the hiring process, one of them did decide to do it.
Darn!

LOST RING

One day going between jobs on my way from college to the parking lot job I lost Nila's class ring. I walked the route twice that day with no luck. It could not be found at the college either. I looked for it every time I went to work, but never did find it, but she was very forgiving.

NILA'S 1954 BLUE FORD Nila had a light blue 1954Ford, a tw0-door. She had her learner's permit and had driven some. I knew not how little. I had started to help her teach the Teens Sunday School Class. One Sunday after Church, she wanted to go down to 3-D Country Store with her car. She did ok turning around in the driveway of her Dad's yard, did ok shifting on the way down, and parked

alright. When we headed home, she took too long going into second gear and did ok the rest of the way
home.

Except as we approached the driveway, her brother was just unloading his car from a two-day fishing trip, he was standing by the open driver's door. Nila got a little flustered and turned into the driveway without shifting into second gear. Les jumped in onto the seat of his car, just before she hit the door slightly. We both heard about that! She sold the car and would not drive for the next four years.

JOINING THE PARTY After 1963, after I had turned 21 (the age required at the time to vote and be active in any Republican Committee), I joined the Standish Republican Committee. I was elected to be a delegate to the Republican

State Convention of which I have been a delegate every two years to date.

I also helped the High School Adviser of the Standish Young Republicans, other committee members helped with the College Republican group.

RALPH MYRON BROOKS III

Went into the Air Force in May of 1963. Training at Lackland Air Force Base in San Antonio, Texas.

His tours took him to:

George AFB in Victorville, CA   Ammo dump

Cuddleback Lake Air to Ground Gunnery Range

Mojave Desert, Death Valley, CA

Forbes AFB in Kansas   Refueling Base

Two Tours of Duty in Vietnam

Ben Hoi AFB in Vietnam and TDY 90 Days in Saigon

Discharged from Randolph AFB in Texas in September 1967.

Total Service Time: 3 yrs. 11 Mos.

d Women In The Service

Returned To States

Airman 3.C. Ralph M. Brooks III, son of Mr. and Mrs. Ralph M. Brooks Jr., Standish, who is stationed at George Air Force Base, Calif. Brooks received his basic training at Lackland AFB, Tex., and has recently spent six weeks in Saigon. He attended Standish and Bonny Eagle High Schools.

CAN SHE COOK?

Spring of 1963 just before classes were over, I got Larry Merrill to skip afternoon classes and drive me to Buxton to surprise Nila. She and her mom were making pies. Besides having flour on her apron, she had some on her nose, on her left cheek and some in her hair.

Surprised yes, but madder at me for skipping classes and catching her all floured up, probably the latter the most. I told her I needed to see if you could cook because I like to eat.

Larry and I made a store run for them and she was cleaned up when we got back. When they were finished, we went for a ride and when we got back to Nila's mom had us stay for supper.

An update on Larry Merrill, after he and Pat were married, they lived in Falmouth for a long time before they moved to Windham. He works for Bodwell Motors.

NILA COOKING

MOM AND NILA SPRING 1963

My mother had a cleaning business in Prout's Neck, Maine. That spring Nila started working with her. My Mother and

Nila got along like mother and daughter and the favorite daughter at that. My Dad was a pushover, he thought we were good for each other.

Finishing my college job early on the last day, I walked to and over the Million Dollar Bridge, hitchhiking Route #77. I walked all the way, no rides that day, taking over five hours, the longest trip to Prout's Neck I ever made. Just barely getting there before Nila and Mom left for home.

By early summer we knew we wanted to get married. I asked her when did you fall in love with me? She replied, "The first night at the dance, but more and more on each date."

By July 4th we were planning the wedding for late August; we went and picked out the rings together. We decided on the last weekend before I started my third year at

Northeastern. So that made the date Saturday August 31, 1963.

We knew that neither set of parents could help with the expenses and we would have to keep a tight rein on the money and pay for it ourselves.

Nila went to the Splended Restaurant where she found a job replacing summer help. We went and found an apartment within walking distance of both.

We planned a Labor Day weekend honeymoon trip to the White Mountains and returning to college the next Tuesday morning.

S.D. WARREN SUMMER OF 1963

The first clean up job was at "Cape Canaveral" a nick name for a building where chemicals were mixed. Chlorine gas was a by-product and sometimes it built up in the recovery lines. It was known for its small explosions. If the alarm went off, you had to run outside. I worked there for two weeks.

The only thing wooden in most of the brick building was the window frames and door jams. I was moved to the paint crew for six weeks. It was two weeks of other painting jobs at Cape Canaveral and then on to other jobs. Then back with the cleaning crew to cover for some of their workers on rotating two-week vacations.

One of the big roof jobs was on a disaster building, three stories up. The old shingles and bad wood had to be lowered to the ground. We did this to free up the carpenters for their next roof job. This was a small roof, to get to it you had to crawl over a desk and out a window.

There was a large steam pipe with a release door that was four feet across, made of heavy plate steel. When the steam was released, the door would lift straight up as the steam blew out fifteen to twenty feet.

There is almost never anyone on that roof, but during this major repair that lasted some ten days, the digester operators had red flags to make sure they warned the crew. I had spoken to the operator on duty before going out that I would be out there alone for the last time, so I left the window open to remind him I was out there.

He still forgot! I had just walked by the steam vent when it went off. I just missed death that time! I came back through the window, diving onto the desk and sliding into his lap, sending papers and charts onto the floor.

My punishment for being frightened to death was to be assigned the "Cell Room" for my last two weeks. The room was always between 100 and 120 degrees all the time. It had large carbon box trays in long lines. The process works the opposite of your car battery, instead of getting energy out they put high electric current into it. The trays have carbon surrounded with a salt brine. When the electricity hits it, there is a chemical break down that gives off a caustic licker and chlorine gas used in paper making; the hydrogen gas was released into the air high above the mill.

This process also coated the trays in sulfur, which had to be washed off daily. To do this you had to be covered head to toe in a rubber suit and use a hose to spray pressurized water on them.

If the chlorine line clogged up, an alarm would sound and you had to evacuate. The chlorine was not good for your health nor would an explosion be. You could not work during a thunderstorm as lightning could set things off. This was a hot two weeks in August, inside and out!

WEDDING PLANS

In July my old Plymouth would not pass inspection. We were saving for our wedding and I could not afford to get a car. I was back to riding with Dad.

Mom picked up Nila on her way to work at Prout's Neck and dropped her off on her way home. Some days Nila would come home with Mom and have supper with us and I would take her home later that gave us time together.

Using Mom's car, we went to Portland and finalized the apartment rental on Pine Street with Mr. and Mrs. Williams. They would take $50.00 off the rent if I would take care of the trash, help put on the storm windows and keep the walkway shoveled, as Mr. Williams was sickly and could not do it.

I paid 10 months' rent in advance, the middle of August to the middle of June, so we would not have to worry about it each month. It would also let us get things moved in early, as we explained the wedding, honeymoon trip and the first day of classes were four days in a row.

We also planned on renting a car for the honeymoon trip but was keeping it a top secret as I was afraid someone would monkey with the car to delay our departure after the reception.

We told everyone that we were using Mom's station wagon, which became well decorated, only my folks and Tim Twombly knew differently. I had Tim's help with that. He drove me into Portland to get the rental car. It was supposed to be a red convertible which was not returned on time; it was being held over. I had to use another car, a new red Ford Fairlane.

I drove the Ford Fairlane to Tim's. We explained to his folks what was going on for they both had to work that weekend and were leaving the car there for the night. Tim was to drive it to the church the next day and park it at the Town Garage which was next door to the church. The cover up was still on.

THE WEDDING

We were getting married in the Buxton Center Baptist Church, the Moulton's home church. Nila's family had it well decorated and the reception goodies all ready. They all walked to the service, as the church was diagonal across the street from their home.

I drove Mom and Dad to the church and parked near the front door.

The church had just changed pastors, Pastor Donald Smith could not make it back, so Pastor Gridley performed the service. The service and reception were just wonderful. When we got ready to leave, after opening the gifts, we walked over to Nila's house to change clothes and get a few things for the trip. We had saved enough to pay for the wedding, but the gifts of money really came in handy on the trip.

Back up a little, at Friday night's rehearsal, Nila's brother Les, one of the ushers, was a little late; at the reception we found out why. He and Gladys had just eloped, getting married by her grandfather, a Notary. They had also thought that Labor Day weekend would make a good time for a honeymoon and, unknown to us all, the White Mountains was their destination also. Our paths did not cross.

If you could have seen their faces when we jumped into a red Ford and took off. My brother Ralph and a few others followed us for a few miles, blowing their horns.

Mom made them undecorate her car before she would drive it home.

Saturday afternoon and evening, we went to go on a cruise on the Mt. Washington Steam Ship on Lake Winnipesaukee. We drove up Route #25 through Limington, Cornish, Kezar Falls, into New Hampshire, Freedom, Center Ossipee, West Ossipee, South Tamworth, East Sandwich, Moultonborough, Moultonborough Falls, and Center Harbor.

The boat had left the dock, but they said, "You have time to drive through Meredith and catch it at Weirs Beach." We made it just before dark with about twenty minutes to spare. We boarded the Mount Washington Cruise Ship and it traveled southeast to Alton Bay, northeast to Wolfboro, northwest up the lake to Center Harbor, and south back to Weirs Beach at about 9:00 P.M.

After the sunset cruise we drove four miles north to Plymouth and stayed at the Woodland Cottages. Mrs. Gray waited on us. Sunday, September 1st, we met Mrs. Gray and her daughter for breakfast. Next, we took a good look at the river next to

Mr. and Mrs. Kenneth R. Brooks

Rev. Robert Gridley Hears Moulton-Brooks Vows

BUXTON — The Buxton Center Church was the scene of the Aug. 31 wedding of Miss Nila Alice Moulton, daughter of Mr. and Mrs. Lesley P. Moulton of West Buxton, and Kenneth Richard Brooks, son of Mr. and Mrs. Ralph M. Brooks Jr. of South Standish. The Rev. Robert Gridley officiated.

THE BRIDE wore a white taffeta gown with lace trim and carried a bouquet of red and white roses.

The maid of honor, Miss Carol Brooks of South Standish, wore a rose taffeta street-length gown and the bride's sister, Miss Nancy Brooks of South Standish and Miss Betty Moulton of West Buxton wore blue taffeta street-length gowns.

LARRY Merrill of South Paris was best man. Ushering were Lesley P. Moulton Jr. of West Buxton and R. Myron Brooks of South Standish.

Following a reception in the Buxton Center Church, the couple left on a trip to Lake Winnipesaukee and through the White Mountains.

The bridegroom is a graduate of Northeastern Business College and has been employed summers by the S. D. Warren Paper Co., Westbrook. The couple will make their home in Portland.

their place took photos before taking in Church Services at the "Old White Church" in Plymouth.

Then we went north on Route #93 to Route #25. We turned left and went five miles to the Polar Caves. I almost got stuck going through a narrow passageway. They had two posts in the ground which you had to pass through as a guide before going in. I think they were a little liberal with that measurement as it was easy; the cave was not!

The pamphlet on the Polar Caves states it's Nature's most spectacular Glacial Rock and Mineral Formation located on Mt. Haycock, fourteen to twenty thousand years old.

We next went to Lost River to another rock formation where the river goes underground for a very long way.

Next, back to Route #93 and going north we stopped at Loon Mountain. They had not opened for the ski season, but they had an old Railroad Engine on display at the entrance of which we took pictures and left.

Next, we came to Clark's Trading Post and their Bear Exhibit. We visited the gift shop and fed the bears.

Up-a-ways and on the left side of the road was Profile Lake with a view of the Indian Head. We used their view finder to look at it on the side of the mountain, a quick stop.

Our next stop was at "The Flume" which we explored for a couple of hours. This is a large brook coming down the side of the mountain. They had constructed a wooden walkway to cross the water over and back in many places. It has miles of small and long waterfalls with stairways to help you climb up in some places. A beautiful place with the fall colors, a picture wonderland.

Late afternoon we stopped at "The Basin" which is at the base of 1900 foot Mt. Franconia. Then up to the north to see a view of the "Old Man of the Mountain"! As it was getting late, we went into the town of Franconia looking for food and lodging.

We found a sign for Sugar Hill, we took a left on Route #117. We stopped at the "Dutch Treat Restaurant" for supper; very good. When asked, they suggested the Coramat Inn and Motel. They said, "Stay on Route #117 and go up to the Chevron Station, turn left and cross the Iron Bridge." The Inn was an old farmhouse with a newer motel next door. The motel was full, but the Inn had one bedroom left with breakfast included.

During the night we could hear the river water running outside our window, upon our arrival we had not noticed, how close, the river was or the small waterfalls below the bridge.

The next morning, Monday September 2nd we had breakfast with the family of the Inn and met another couple. Mr. and Mrs. Brent Robinson were newlyweds from Canada and Massachusetts. When we left, we drove down through Bethlehem and Bethlehem Junction on our way to Brenton Woods, Crawford Notch, and the Silver Cascade. The Notch is at 1,773 feet, with the Mountains in the 4,000-foot range all around. These are the other Mountains that surround the Notch.

Mt. Hancock	4,403
Mt. Currigan	4,580
Mt. Liberty	4,459
South Twin Mts	4,902
Mt. Deception	3,658
Mt. Adams	5,774

Mt. Eisenhower	4,760
Middle Carter Mtn.	4,584
West Royce Mtn.	3,116
Mt. Parker	3,015

We stopped to see the Willey House and the Railroad Station House. They are located beside the tracks overlooking Route #302 at Crawford Notch and above Arethusa Falls. Then we traveled through Bartlett, Glen, Intervale, and into North Conway for lunch. Heading home through Conway turning onto Route #153 through Eaton Center, and in Madison we stopped at "King Pine Ski Resort", again not open. Next stop was in Freedom at my Grandparents Ralph and Hattie Brooks for a short visit. The last stop for sightseeing was the covered bridge on Route #160 in Porter, Maine.

Stopped at my dad and Moms for a quick visit so they would know that we were home safe. Then Nila's Dad and Moms for the same reason. That's when they told us that after the rehearsal Les, Jr. and his new wife Gladis Churchill had

Spent the night in a motel in South Portland by the mall before coming to our wedding.

We returned the car in Portland and they gave us a ride to our new apartment and the landlords 14-pound cat Mittens was on guard duty.

MITTENS

The next day I started my 3rd year at Northeastern, and Nila started at the

Splended Restaurant a few days later.

NORA, FALL OF 1963 AT SPLENDED RESTAURANT

Nora was very nice and helped Nila get used to her new job. Nora had just found a new boyfriend. In a few months they got married and he took a new job in Massachusetts, so off they went.

Ingred, a Norwegian Immigrant, worked there; we got to meet her husband and two boys. They lived on Franklin Street (now the Franklin Arterial) and he worked at the fish pier and market where the fishing boats came in.

Nila worked the supper shift at the restaurant and during the day took a course at the Maine Medical Center to become a nurse's aide. When she graduated, she left the restaurant and worked at the hospital from 3 to 11. I worked after my college classes at the college from 3 to 4:30 and the parking lot from 5 to 7. That left 7:30 to 10:30 pm for the four of us (the study group) to meet and do homework. After I showed them out of the apartment I walked up to the hospital and walked Nila home. Then we had supper.

"If you're hungry enough, you'll eat and if you'er tired enough, you'll sleep. The problem is getting up on time to start it all over again.

THE STUDY GROUP

Larry Merrill, Jimmie Ryan, Don Meserve, and myself. The first time was at Larry's apartment, but we all found that it was too small; it was easier at mine.

CHARLES AND PAM CROMWELL

Pam and Nila went to grade school at what is now the Dunston School House Restaurant in Scarborough before the Moulton's moved to Buxton. We all visited a few times as we all were living on Pine Street at the time, even went out to eat once.

Then one night on my way home from the parking lot job, Pam was trying to get Charlie home after a bar visit and a few too many. I helped her get him up to their second-floor apartment.

PRESIDENT KENNEDY'S ASSASSINATION

November 22, 1963, after classes, I had finished cleaning up the college rooms and I was headed for the parking lot job. As I was going down the front granite steps, a lady in the next-door apartment building lifted the window and leaned out hollering that President Kennedy had been shot. I did a lot of thinking on the way to work.

The State Street Catholic Church owned the parking lot where I worked. In the forty's when car parking came into being, they had bought a house behind the church, tore the building down and made it into a parking lot for the church parking on Sundays. They rented parking spaces Monday through Saturdays and hired a member of the church, Chales Saunders, to manage the parking lot for whom I worked. This gave them an extra income.

When I got there, I met an older priest who was most upset by the turn of events about which we had a long conversation about the national tragedy. He had lost his catholic president.

TEACHING TYPING

In the winter of 1963 Mrs. Sullivan, the typing teacher, fell and broke her hip. Well, I had two years of typing in high school and two in college. The Principal Mr. Myron Libby came to me and asked me to fill in. I said, "Me, a teacher?" The faculty thought that I qualified to substitute as a class monitor passing out her assignments and instructing the features of the typewriter. Her recovery lasted four months. I got good praises from the faculty and the students, as well as looking good on my resume.

NAT KING COLE

One day while working at the parking lot, Larry Merrill had me come over to the hotel so I could meet Nat King Cole when he came in on his tour bus. A very tall, classy gentleman. As he got off the bus, I was able to shake his very large hand and received a warm welcome.

BOWLING AND SUNDAY AFTERNOON WALKS

When we lived on Pine Street, Nila and I would walk down to the corner of Congress and High Streets to the bowling alley. After bowling a while, we would walk down and back up the other side of Congress Street looking into all the store front windows at their displays.

A NEW DRESS FOR NILA

One Sunday at Learners, a Ladies Clothing Store, in their display window we saw a red dress with matching shoes.

During the week I went back alone and they were taking the display down. I went in to see about the sizes; they both were size five which was Nila's size. Her feet were so small she always had to buy the small mannequin shoes. Needless to say, I bought them and then had to keep them hid until Valentine's Day.

Nila thought that I should not have spent the money, but she quickly gave me a big hug and a long kiss. She wore them to several Republican Events.

THE YELLOW TIE

Fritzy Coyne an Employee of a T.V. station in a building on the corner of Congress Street and High Street in Portland. It was within walking of the parking lot. She was usually the last customer to leave for the day. For Christmas 1963 Fritzy Coyne gave me another tie. A nice yellow one with a Christmas wreath on it. I had it for many years.

THE MOVE AROUND THE CORNER

Eight months into our rental on Pine Street, our landlord Mrs. Florence Williams lost her husband and had to sell the house. We were given a lot of very nice furniture for the two month's rent we had prepaid. A very nice deal; we kept it and used it for many years.

We moved to the Carlton Street Apartments, an adult facility, no children allowed.

THE THIRD JOB INTERVIEW

Just before college was out King Cole Foods Potato Chip and Candy Company called the college looking for another student. As John Lord was leaving after just one year, I went and interviewed and got the job. I had a job to go to; I returned to college and finished up.

I graduated from Northeastern Business College with a bachelor's degree in accounting.

I started just after the 4th of July 1964 at $45.00 a week. Gas was $.30 a gallon and milk was $.48 a gallon. I had to walk six blocks to catch the bus to Cash Corne in South Portland. Then walk down Cash Street two blocks to the office. The bus schedule made it so that I had to start a little late and work a little late to make up.

Jack Hays was the owner.

William Kelly (Bill) Officer Manager
Wife Nyla (same name different spelling)

Mary Smith   Cashier

Kenn Brooks   Business Machine Operator

Kenny Fuller   Farm Manager

Bill did up all the worksheets, Payroll,

Accounts Payable, Accounts Receivable

Mary cashed up each Route Salesman and what products he had sold.

Kenn took the worksheets and entered them on the Remington Rand bookkeeping machine.

The machine looked like a giant combined typewriter/adding machine keyboard, but with different carriage bars, which were interchangeable, with tab stops set up differently.

Each activity had its own program.

The sales tracker was the hardest one and took the most time. All route salespeople and their sales by each product category. They were getting to where they needed a computer.

Kenny Fuller worked at the farm in Buxton where they raised some of their own potatoes. One winter day, on my way to work, I went off the road. It was snowing hard. A school bus was making a stop as it was approaching in the opposite direction. When I went to stop, I started sliding right toward the bus.

Finally slowing down and getting better traction I got back on my side of the road, but kept going up onto the snowbank.

I got a ride to work and called Don Baker; he got there with his wrecker before the cops got there, took the car to his shop and checked it out; nothing was broken.

I worked nights for a while because there was no way to keep up on that antiquated machine. I would go down to Lano's Restaurant at Cash Corner for supper, then go back and work for two hours extra. I got to know the family; one of their sons was killed in Vietnam.

CINERAMA (A TRADEMARK)

Cinerama' is a motion picture which gives the illusion of being three dimensional. A three-lens camera, a curved cycloramic screen, three projectors, and dimensional sound are employed to produce the illusion. Two years later, they had perfected a new Cinerama lens that works like our eye.

Cinema (short for cinematography) Motion pictures collectively or a motion picture theater.

"MAD, MAD, MAD WORLD"

After college was out Jimmy and Dorothy Ryan invited Nila and I to go to Boston with them to see the movie, "Mad, Mad, Mad World" on the new Cinerama Screen. On a 1964 summer weekend, we went to the big city. Jim was driving and he took a wrong street and had to turn around. The next side street had a railroad track in the middle of it, he turned in and the train was coming! Had to back into a driveway to make a quick exit. We laughed over it for years as Dotty was so startled at the sight of the engine coming right at us.

The movie was the funniest I ever saw; it kept us all laughing throughout the entire movie. The color and Cinerama effects were just great, and when up in a plane

JIM AND DOROTHY RYAN

you could see the circumference of the earth.

The second Cinerama movie was "The 7 Wonders of the World".

WILLARD BEACH

One Sunday we took a trip by city bus to Willard Beach, enjoyed the sun and swam in the ocean. Neither of us had done it before and did not know we should shower before the long bus ride home.

We felt the effects of the salt water; I was so chafed, I never did swim in the ocean again.

CLYDE AND DOROTHY WADLE

They lived in Tamaqua, Pennsylvania and belonged to the Mennonite Church. They came to Maine so Clyde could fulfill his 1-W service as a Conscientious Objector, with which I never had a problem with. They are nice people and have become good friends. The next two paragraphs are from a letter from Dorothy, she says:

CLYDE AND DOROTHY WADLE

"We went to Maine May 12, 1964. Clyde started working at Maine Medical Center on May 18th. He worked in House Keeping 1 week before beginning training for orderly work on May 25th. We took training together and we think Nila was the only other girl in the class, tho there was a boy too. Training was for 3 weeks, 2 weeks training before we were on the floor with supervisor oversight. Then we were on our own with the nurses help where needed. Clyde was assigned to

BSurgical second floor of the old hospital and I was on P2A, second floor of the new part of the hospital. Nila and I worked on this floor together. Our jobs were to give baths, pass out drinks morning and afternoon, record intake and output, set up and pass out dinner trays, and help anyone who needed help to eat, sometimes feeding them. Heart attack patients were not allowed to do anything for themselves We were taught how to prepare a body for the morgue, and take them down, tho I only remember doing that one time. Clyde remembers going to the morgue, more especially when he worked in Escort Service. We were taught how to take care of isolation patients too." "I remember Nila (Brooks) passing out drinks and she even made a "Pink Lady Drink." I think it was orange juice and cranberry juice. I remember she was a good worker and not afraid to help where needed. She worked *longer than I did before the birth of our girls. She just got bigger uniforms!"*

Kaylene Wadle   May 12, 1965

Annette Brooks   Sept. 5, 1965

Signed Dorothy Wadel

NANCY – HOW I MET RAY

In February 1964 Nancy Brooks was a sophomore at Bonny Eagle High School in Standish, Maine. Raymond Reitze, Jr. was a junior, but they had the same biology class and he sat in the back of the room. Nancy said, "He was very shy, spoke very little, a quiet dude."

Nancy went to most of the school dances. The Valentines dance actually fell on February 14, 1964.

Ray, not having a driver's license, was riding with his friend George Gibbs. Ray got up his courage and asked Nan for a dance, the beginning of their story. The Brooks lived a mile from the school and Nancy had to walk to the dance. When Ray learned Nan had to walk home, they offered that they could take her home. Nacy said, "I took them up on their offer as she felt safe with them."

RAYMOND REITZE, JR.

Ray walked her to the door and before he said goodnight, he asked her to wear his ring. In those days boys and girls would swap rings and wear them on a chain around their neck – as a sign you were "going steady". Nancy said, "I didn't know how long it would last."

They got engaged in 1965 and married on April 7, 1966. They had two girls, Lenore and April. They are still happily married.

AL & CAROL'S WEDDING 7/18/64

My sister Carol's wedding to Joseph Paul Albert John Archambault, a.k.a., (Al) was at St. Anne's Catholic Church in Gorham, Maine.

The Best Man was Mike Sullivan, a.k.a. (Sully). The Maid of Honor was Nancy Marston. The Ushers were Tom Wiley and Kenn Brooks.

Al's best friend in the Canadian Air Force, Sully flew down from Canada and stayed in Portland. We all liked him and he was a big help getting things ready, even helping making flowers to decorate the hall and Al's car. The flowers were made from tissue paper.

The reception was held in the Grand Army of the Republic Hall next door to our house in Standish, Maine.

AL's DECORATED CAR

Nancy Brooks caught the bouquet and Raymond Reitze, Jr. caught the garter (see previous photo).

Carol and Al had a honeymoon trip up the Maine coast as far as Rockport. After the main trip, they were off to Sioux Lookout Ontario, Canada. It was a joint American/Canadian Air Force Base on the D.E.W. Line. They were watching for possible Russian attack by airplane or by missiles.

BOWLING

Nila and I went bowling at Prides Corner Lanes several times and always had a good time. Then another young couple asked if we would be interested in joining a couple's league that they were starting. It turned into a wonderful time for us.

We both got better with averages of 110 and 130 and I worked it up some. I even started with the big balls and joined a men's league.

I got good enough to stay on the team another year, but when Annette was born, we had to give it up because of the lack of time and money.

KENN WORKING ON FAMILY BOOKKEEPING

JOKES

1. "The difference between death and taxes is that death doesn't get worse every time congress meets." By Will Rogers.

2. "The goal isn't to live forever; the goal is to create something that will."

3. "Life is likening to a card game, the couple with two Hearts, then comes a Diamond. Years later one of them is looking for a Club and a Spade."

4. The old guy goes to the doctors. Doc wants to know how he is doing. Why I'm doing fine, but you know of late when I go to the bathroom the light comes on and when I'm done it goes off.

5. Doc thinks he'll have to check this story out. When the wife comes in for her appointment, he asked her about the light?

Oh, he's been going to the refrigerator again.

The cop stopped an old guy in an old truck for not using his turn signal when he turned onto the old country lane. Well sir, everyone around here knows my truck and that is where I live here.

6. The teacher asked Johnny how much is four and four? He looks at his hands and says eight. Yes, but I don't want you to count your fingers, now put your hands in your pockets and tell me how much is five and five?
Johnny looks up at the ceiling and rolls his eyes and says, "Eleven."

7. Three women went up to see St. Peter. He wanted to know how they died: first woman said she had a heart attack; second woman said she died in a car accident, and the third woman said she had V.D. "You can't die from V.D." "Oh yes, you can when you give it to Elroy."

8. On the next day he asked three what they did for work. One said a teacher, two said a school bus driver, and three said she was the CEO of the local HMO.. Well, I have to think about that one. Well, O.K. you can go in with the other two, but you can only stay three days.

9. The. Chicken farmer was going down the road stops and gets out and takes a baseball bat and hits the side of the truck just as a cop comes around the corner. The cop follows him down the road and the farmer stops and hits the truck again. The cop pulls in and says, "I don't see anything wrong with your driving. The truck looks OK, but why are you hitting the truck with a baseball bat?" "Well, officer, you know this is a one-ton truck, and I have three ton of birds on board, so I must keep two ton of them flying at all times."

QUOTES

A. "Life by the yard, is awfully hard,

But inch by inch, it's a cinch"

An Irish one

B. "May your pockets be heavy, and your heart be light.

May good luck pursue you each morning and night.

May happiness and good luck surround you.

C. Wherever you wander, whatever you do."
In your journeys to and fro, may God DIRECT thee;

D. in thy happiness and pleasure, may God BLESS thee; in care and anxiety and trouble, may God SUSTAIN thee; in peril and danger, may God PROTECT thee.

YEAR 1965

I joined the Standish Republican Committee. The oldest member and chairman, Bryon Waterman challenged me to raise money in my district I went the length of Rive Road, door to door, and beat him by $15.00. He had three donations of $25.00. I got $10.00 from a democrat that said, "That he never saw anyone from his party come door to door." I had 16 at $5.00 for $80.00 plus the $10.00.

I was a delegate to the Republican State Convention that year and every two years since except last year (2020) because of COVID-19 it was done online. I'm the convention chairperson for Standish for April 30,2022.

JANUARY 1965 THE BABY IS COMING

Nila didn't want me or anyone else to get excited before it was confirmed, so, she made an appointment with one of the hospital Gynecologists. Yes, she was expecting, and yes, we were overjoyed.

Then it sank in, we were going to have to move, as we were living in an adult facility, no children allowed, and we had no car. I was riding the city bus to work, and the South Portland connections were terrible at the time and the economy was bad.

Mom and Dad Brooks wanted to see us, so Mom made arrangements to pick us up for the weekend. We told them about the baby that was coming, and that we had to move because of it.

Mom said, 'That was not all the bad news, the mill was going on short time, Dad was going on a four-day workweek. They would not be able to make the house payments."

After a couple of weekends, "work sessions" we decided to move back home at the end of the summer. The baby was not due until September. Mom and Nila would be out of work at Prouts Neck, I could use her car to go, back and forth, to work at King Cole Foods in South Portland for the winter.

Dad, Charlie Link, and Ralph Damond were going to carpool to the Westbrook Mill to help on the gas bill for everyone. A couple of times when they had car problems, they got a ride with Robert Wyman or Emery Wills which was not the best way. It did not work well because Bob and Emery worked on the other side of the mill, which was on the other side of the Presumpscot River and Emery worked tower shifts. It usually got them to work, but not home.

Nila and I planned on getting a car before spring when the girls would start at Prouts Neck again. I went to see Don Baker at Wass Garage to see about a car. He had an older customer that was going to sell his Chevy, two-tone, tan and brown station-wagon, which I did buy.

AFTER THE MOVE HOME

After we got to Standish with Dad and Mom, we would work Saturdays on the joint projects with Dad and Mom Brooks. I would help in the garden or on firewood with Dad. Nila would help Mom in the house, or we all would work harvesting the garden and canning the crops. On Sundays, we would go to the Buxton Center Baptist Church, teach Sunday School, go to the Church service and go over with Dad and Mom Moulton for dinner, and for an afternoon visit. There was always Nila's four younger siblings, Betty Ann, Kenneth, Nancy, and Janice. We went back to Brooks for supper.

RALPH DAMON

ANNETTE MARIE

Annette was born on September 5, 1965. The pregnancy was an easy one, but at the end Nila drove Mom crazy, mostly the last day, as she was not in any hurry to head to the hospital. When we left, Mom said to me, "Don't waste any time getting there." I didn't, in fact, I hurried.

When I pulled up to the emergency entrance, they brought out a wheelchair, and Nila's water broke moving her from the car to the wheelchair. She delivered as they put her on the table, Doctor not in the room. That was too close for me. I was fond of the name Annette, from the T.V. show the Three Mousketeers, Annette Funicello, an easy sell as Nila liked it too.

When we brought the baby home, that was when the problems started with thirteen-year-old Chester. Nila put him in his place a couple of times, with mother's support.

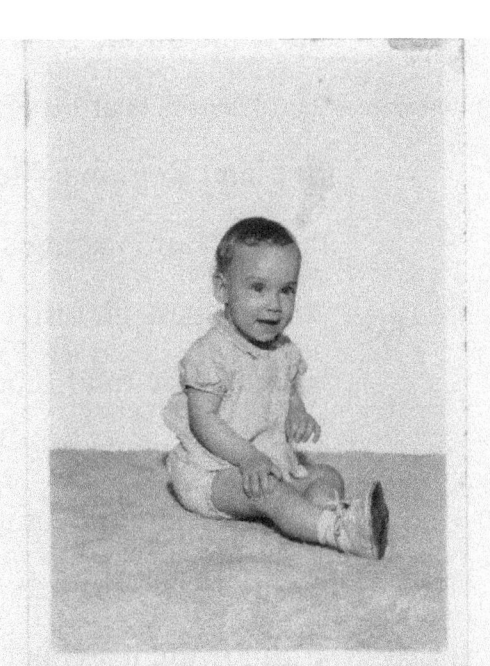

NANCY'S GYMNASTICS MEET IN SPRINGFIELD, MASSACHUSETTS

At the State Meet my sister Nancy was the only one on the Bonny Eagle High School gymnastics team to qualify to the New England Regional Meet. She did well in her division placing second on the uneven parallel bars and first in the "All Around" which is the total score for all four events. The four events were: Floor Exercise, Vault, Balance Beam, and the Uneven Parallel Bars. Her first place on the "All around" qualified her to go to the New England Regional Gymnastics Meet which was in Springfield, Massachusetts.

Mom wanted to go. The school was not sending anyone else or a bus. Mom asked me if I would drive her and Nancy way out there with her car. Plans were made and we left really early that morning and made it with some 40 minutes to spare.

It was interesting to watch, Nancy was impressed at how advanced the next division was. Nancy did not place in the event.

On the way home late at night a fox ran into us. How he got across four lanes of traffic into the median strip I don't know. I was in the third lane and a car in the fourth passing lane was about to go by us, when the fox bolted out of the median strip, crossed in the lights of the passing car and into my left front wheel. This threw him back into the path of that car. I took my foot off the gas, but with the cars all around me, I realized in time not to try to stop, and went back to the gas pedal. We got home late and tired.

After almost 3 months at boot camp in Fort Dix, N.J. Raymond Reitze had been sent to Loring Air Force Base in Limestone, Maine. He spent his time on TDY duty at the Missile Base in Caribou,

Maine working on generators for the power system. Then Ray got orders to go to Fort Hancock in New Jersey. Their Wedding date changed three times. Ray

NANCY AND RAYMOND REITZE, JR.

and Nancy got married before Nancy's graduation. Nancy said, "The coach was unhappy she got married, because the coach thought she was good enough to work to compete in the Olympic tryouts.

CINDY

Ray had a palomino horse named Cindy. Ray bought her in 1961 from Sonny and Eunis Oleson in Westbrook, Maine. She was 2 years old, and she was full of it, so Ray had her bred. I met and started going with Ray while she was carrying. She had a colt which we sold a year later. They had to find her a temporary home while they were in New Jersey. Good friends and neighbors of Ray's, Ernest and Coralee Kinny said they would love to keep her until he got out of the service. We took Cindy to Harrison when we moved there. Took her to Standish while we lived in the trailer at Dad and Mom's, then to Canaan in 1980 when we bought the farm. We had to put her down a year or two later when she got kicked by another horse in a fight. We had taken in, to help a girl out who needed a place for her horse because her folks filed for a divorce, and they were renting in a trailer

park next to us. A bad mistake on our part, Cindy was about 23 years old.

After graduation Al and Carol (Brooks) Archambault took Nancy to be with Ray in Fort Hancock, N.J. Ray was there in the motor pool when he got his orders for Viet Nam in September of 1967.

STANDISH FIRE DEPARTMENT

In 1966 I joined the fire department at Station One at Standish Corner. I started with forest fire training and how to use the "Indian Tank" which you carried on your back to put water on the fire, when empty you went back for a refill.

Next, they tried to teach me to get water out of the pumper truck, it was too complicated, which lever was first, how long to wait to start the next step. I just could not get the routine. I was not good at First Aid. I could not get a victim's pulse or evaluate other problems.

I served as the treasurer for three years and set up a book of the fire ponds, the rivers, or brooks that were in each area, such as the underground storage tank at "Cabbage Yard" at the junction of Route #35 and Dow Road, that was put in by the neighborhood for their own protection.

RICHARD ALIN

We were still at the farm on September 23, 1966, when Richard was born. A repeat performance, Nila was slow to leave, another quick ride. This time we made the delivery room right at the time of a shift change. A nurse had me sit in the antcroom and then she went home. No husbands in the delivery room in those days. Nila delivered within five minutes of being on the table, again before the doctor could get into the room. Then nobody knew that I was in the waiting room, my mother got a call before I went to the desk to inquire, "We were looking

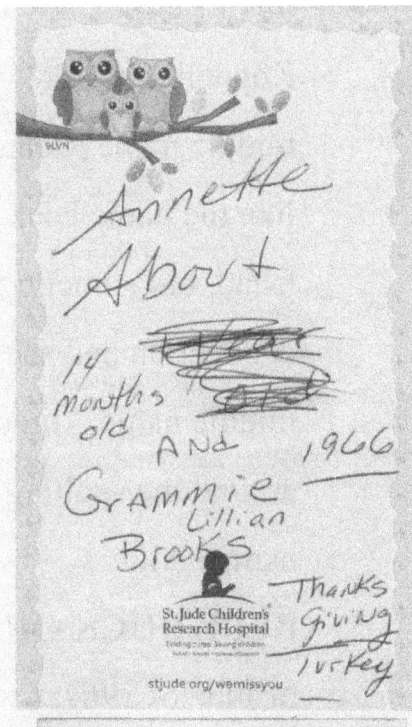

for you." Well, you didn't look in the obvious place. We had talked about names, Nila wanted to name a boy after me, I said, "There is not going to be a Kenneth, Jr." So, we settled on my middle name Richard. We both did not like the name Dick, so we tried to call him Chad, but Annette could not get the connection and she made it Rich. The middle name Alin came from turning around the spelling of Nila, so he was named Alin.

BLUE ROCK QUARRY

In June of 1967, I went to work for the Blue Rock Quarry at $54.00 a week ($1.35 an hour).. They were owned by the same people as W.H.Hinman Construction Company The office crew was divided up every other Saturday morning. One person had to come in an hour early every six weeks to cover the switchboard from 7:00 am to 8:00 am.

The regular operator then would come on duty for the remainder of the day.

Buck Wyman
 Personnel Manager and Treasurer

Doris Worster
 Office Mgr. and Accounts Receivable

Robert Webster
 Truck Supervisor

Steven Manen
 Accounts Payable

Raymond Weeks
 Accounts Payable

Kenn Brooks
 Payable & Accounts Payable

Edward Cabral
 Payroll

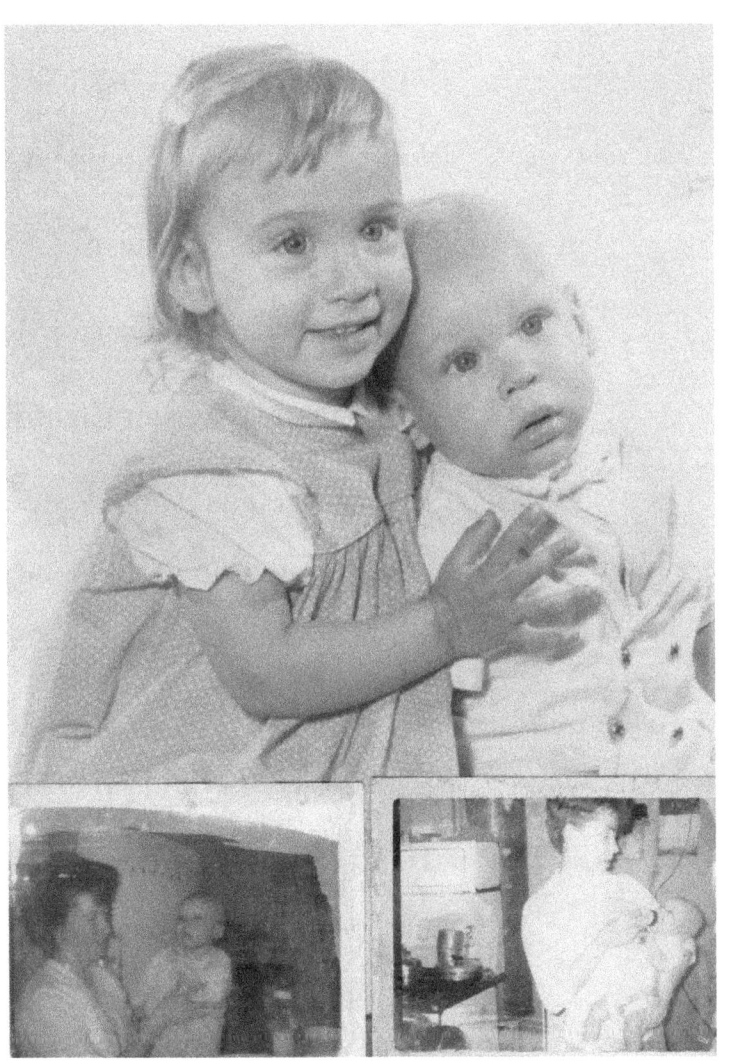

Joan Merrill-Weeks   Comp Programmer

Carol Dice   Computer Operator

Carolyn Burrows   Switchboard Operator

Jim Hinman   Engineer

Lloyd Lathrop   Engineer

Robert Nunly Supervisor Concrete Plant

Norman Stone Supervisor Paving Plant

Al Sampson   Master Electrician

I first worked as a bookkeeper taking care of payroll and hours for the equipment. You had to be sure that the employees were paid overtime correctly, and their time charged to the proper job also.

  That the equipment was billed out at the right rate for each and to the job or charged as idle time.

To make it more difficult, Federal Jobs at the airport and I-95, the employees were paid O.T. after 8 hours in a day, state jobs were paid O.T. after 40 hours in a week.

Another thing that made it harder was some employees were moved around and worked on each type of job in a week and yes some on both in one day.

On one of those special Saturday mornings, I had got the switchboard up and running. The first call was a nurse at Maine Medical Center, if, you can find Mr. Robershaw's thumb and get it in here, we can sew it back on, clink.

I'm going to explain how I knew what to do, the process to solving the problem, and how I found out which timekeeper to call.

There were two of us that worked in the payroll department at the time and two others who had been promoted to other jobs. Four out of 26 who could easily solve this problem. The foremen of each job sent in the timecards at the end of the day. Seven to twelve jobs going at any time. Most of the time, but not always the employee would start out at the job he left the night before. I knew that Mr. Robershaw was the head mechanic and followed the equipment from place to place. I quickly went and collected all the timecards and sorted through them until I found Mr. Robershaw's, he had worked the last two hours at the Airport job. I placed a call to the timekeeper at the Airport and told him the problem. End of story the mechanic had been working on an old Steam Shovel, while greasing it his glove caught in the turning gear, the glove and thumb were found and sent to the hospital and the surgery was successful.

You guessed it, no thank you for that one.

FARMERS HOME ADMINISTRATION

In 1967 I was in the Standish Jaycees and a fellow member Alton Wedburg was a loan originator for the Farmers Home Administration for Cumberland County.

He said it was hard to get a house qualified for the program, that the best way was to find a house for sale with that kind of mortgage already. I didn't make it any easier because I wanted to stay in Standish as I was already getting into town affairs, the Jaycees, the Fire Department, and the Republican Town Committee. There were few in Cumberland County and the competition was stiff, and the only house in Standish was down in Sebago Lake Village by the Gorham town line. Alton worked hard to get us into that two-bedroom house.

Heads Jaycees

Kenneth R. Brooks has been elected president of Sebago - Standish Jaycees. Other new officers are Norman Foster, Sebago, internal vice president; Jay Bertin, external vice president; Edward Haggerty, secretary and treasurer; and Edward Richards, state director. (Vic Richards Photo)

THE SEBAGO-STANDISH JAYCEES

This club is set up to make young men future leaders in their community with an age limit of 21 to 36 years old. Larry Simpson was the president, and the meetings were held in his gift shop at Long Beach.

They had a "Speak Up Program" which was a big help to me. You had to speak one minute about yourself. Then three minutes about your favorite subject. Next five minutes about something they pick in advance, you have a week to prepare for it. The last one was for two to three minutes. They called you up and gave you a subject to speak about cold turkey. I do not remember what my subject was. The funniest one was done by David Stocks about how to light a cigarette, open the package, take it out, tap the end, put it in your mouth, taking a match and striking it to light it up, and then puffing on it until you choke. His acting performance was just so funny.

In 1968 I was Club President, and Larry Simpson was president of the Maine State Jaycees, and Birch Dunn was the Vice President. That year we changed the club's name to just Standish Jaycees. We also sponsored a Little League Team. We called it The Jaycees and I was the coach.

Our members were Jay Bertin, Kenn Brooks, Mike Delcourt, John Driscall, Norman Foster, Edward Haggerty, Edward Richards, Larry Simpson a JCI Senator, David Stocks, Larry Stocks, Raymond Staples, Veto Umbro, Allen Wedberg. Other clubs and members we had good times with. Buxton- Hollis Cliff Rollins, Erland Townsend – Falmouth Gary Reed a JCI Senator – Fort Fairfield Peter Hunt – Gorham Ralph and Sheila Berry, Wayne Worster – Hampden Birch Dunn – Rockland Bruce Saunders.

For several years our fund raiser was a cider sale. We got permission to sell the cider at Bill and Hazel Dow's Farm Stand on Route 25 in Standish where Family Dollar is now. The best time was Fryberg Fair Week.

We went around to get glass gallon jugs and wash them. We went to several apple orchards to get apple drops and take everything to Hawk Cider Press in Windham. We would be there on Saturday morning to help at the press and bring it back to Dow's.

We also decided to try to go from three to five selectmen. We got up a partition and enough signatures to get it on the ballot, but we lost by a small margin. I also helped make up the letterhead with the outline of Sebago Lake faintly in the background.

The Jaycees moved our meetings to the Town Hall. I hit the age limit of 36 in

In Loving Memory of

Erlon Lawrence Townsend
1941-2014

Dennett, Craig and Pate Funeral Homes
Robert D. Pate · James T. Pate · Chad E. Poitras

Erlon Lawrence Townsend, 72

Erlon Lawrence Townsend

BUXTON — Erlon Lawrence Townsend, 72, of Pennell Road, died unexpectedly on May 28, 2014, at the Maine Medical Center in Portland.

Erlon was a lifelong Buxton resident and worked throughout his life as a farmer. He was active in the community with the Buxton Fire Dept. and most recently served with the Buxton Fire Police.

He is survived by his children, Andy of Buxton, Linda of Buxton, Steven of Buxton, and Tony and his wife Cheryl of Porter; sister, Sally Rohl of New York; and eight grandchildren.

Visiting hours will be on Saturday morning, May 31, from 9-10:30 a.m., at the Dennett, Craig & Pate Funeral Home, Rts 202 and 4A in Buxton. A graveside service will follow at approximately 11 a.m. at South Buxton (Tory Hill) Cemetery. Everyone then is invited to attend a reception at the Buxton (Bar Mills) Fire Station. www.dcpate.com.

In lieu of flowers, memorial contributions can be made to:
The Buxton Fire Dept.
185 Portland Rd.
Buxton, Maine 04093

Raymond Staples Sr., 75

STANDISH – Raymond Staples Sr., 75, of Standish, passed away Nov. 7, 2017.

He was born on Nov. 21, 1941, the son of John B. and Catherine A. (Dugan) Staples.

Ray grew up in Worcester, Mass., and graduated from Commerce High School. He attended post-secondary school and enrolled in the United States Coast Guard, where he served for four years. On Sept. 1, 1967, he married Jean Hannaford and together they moved to Maine where they made their home and raised their family. Ray was employed at Vermont as an equipment installer until his retirement.

Throughout the years, Ray was heavily involved with several local civic organizations, including the Junior Chamber of Commerce, public safety volunteer, Cub Master of the Boy Scouts, and especially the Kiwanis Club of Standish. A man of few words, Ray enjoyed supporting the local high school sports teams, watching the races at Bench Ridge and going for long drives. Ray also loved spoiling his beloved dog, Bode.

He is survived by his loving wife of 50 years, Jean Staples, of

January 1978, being with the Jaycees for 10 years in and just before the National Jaycees voted to include women members. They now outnumber men in some clubs.

CHESTER AND RUTH (SHAW) SEALS

Chester was my garage mechanic and car salesman for about eight years. He and his wife Ruth became close friends. I was an Amway Salesman at the time. She became one of my Amway customers. I spent many an evening talking with them, on many different subjects. His son Chester Seals, Jr. worked for Dad for years before taking a job at S.D. Warren Paper Co. in their equipment garage. He later started a garage of his own, as his brother-in-law Gary Nelson had started running Chet's Auto Sales.

At this time, Nila took Driver's Ed with a private company and got her license.

HUNTING WITH LESLEY MOULTON JR.

Les and Gladys lived on Pigeon Brook Road in Baldwin, Maine with the Mountain Division Railroad tracks running right at the edge of their backyard. When you cross the RR tracks the land drops down to the floor plain along the Saco River. There was a large field with woods on each end and timber land on the other side of the river.

Les had gotten a couple of his big bucks there in the past. On this day we walked miles back and forth, but this day the deer alluded us.

In the fall of 1968, Les took me up to Athens, Maine to a place he liked to hunt. It was an old farm with land running up to the base of a mountain. We went in a longways on a three-wheeler; he dropped me off in an area where a brook ran into a bog. There was a high bank on one side of the road which made a nice blind. He went halfway up the mountain and parked the three-wheeler.

He always liked to hunt alone, because as he said, "That way you could breathe in the woods deeper." He covered a lot of ground and finely jump two deer and they came down the brook on my side. The big buck went right across the brook and onto the mountain. The doe came my way, I could hear her jumping and getting closer, I could not see her, and I began to climb up the bank for a better view. If she had not detected my movement and changed course a little bit, she would have leapt right over me when she jumped onto the roadway. By the time I got turned around she was making her exit into the woods. He covered a lot of ground and finally jumped two deer and they came down the brook on my side. The big buck went right across the brook and up onto the mountain. The doe came my way. I could hear her jumping and getting closer, I could not see her, and I began to climb

BIG BUCK — Lesley Moulton of West Baldwin shows off the nine-point, 299-lb buck he dropped with one shot from his bow and arrow. Lesley has an official dressed weight of 229 lbs which qualifies him for the Biggest Buck in Maine Club. Moulton got his buck during a special Bow and Arrow shoot. (UPI)

up the bank for a better view. If she had not detected my movement and changed course a little bit, she would have leaped right over me when she jumped into the roadway. By the time I got turned around she was making her exit into the woods.

Les had seen an area on the mountain where a buck had been spending a lot of time. He made a bee line there and claimed a large Hemlock tree and was waiting when "Mr. Buck" came through. After dressing the 10-point, 200 lb. prize, he went and got the three-wheeler. He parked on the downhill side and managed to get the older feller loaded. He was some proud when he picked me up just before dark for the long ride out. The transfer of "Mr. Buck" from the threewheeler to the truck was a chore. We had a good trip to the tag station and home.

Standish Pastor Nam[ed]
Outstanding Young M[an]

Roger William Braley
January 12, 1941–September 14, 2017

*I have fought the good fight
I have finished the race,
I have kept the faith. 2 Timothy 4:7*

SEBAGO LAKE CONGREGATIONAL CHURCH

Nila and I joined the Church December 19, 1968 and Norman Rust was the Pastor. Then Roger (Bill) Braley was well-liked and grew the Church membership. When Larry and June Simpson joined it seemed no one wanted to sit down front, they would start to fill up from the last pew working forward. Larry said to me "Let's move our families down front." And, we did. Then, others started to fill in behind us.

Nila and Andrea Yates joined the Sunday School staff and the classes grew. When we had enough teens I taught that class. After three years, Nila became the Sunday School

Superintendent. I was a Deacon, a Trustee, and sang in the choir. The Church was part of a three Church parish, the Minister had to do three services, Baldwin at 9:00 am, Standish at 10:00 am, and Sebago Lake at 11:00 am. I also became the Treasurer of the Three Church Parish for several years.

Nila and I wanted to go to Bible Study, and she got her younger sister Janice to babysit the kids. The first night we had been there only a little while when we got a call that Richard had fallen out of the Beech tree on the ftont lawn. We had to take him to Emergency Care for a broken arm. We were active in the Church until the kids headed off to college.

One time at Grandpa Brooks' when Uncle John and Aunt Lucy and the twin girls were there for a visit, I was going to take Dad and John to the store and Annette and Richard wanted to go. We had them get into the hatchback of the little Ford Pinto. It did not close tight and when I sarted off the hatch opened when Richard leaned against it and as he rolled out onto the drivewya, Annette was yelling, "Stop! Stop! Richard fell out!" He got up and brushed himself off, he was not hurt.

On a visit to his grandparents, the Moulton's, Richard was playing on the piano stool, and it fell over as he got off of it and hit his toe and cut a little of the end of it off. Emergency Room again!

MILK FROM JACK GORDON (1-251947 to 12-13-2020)

I was looking for a place to buy raw milk. I went to the two dairy farms on Mighty Street in Gorham about three miles away. The Clark family did not want to do it. Robert and Phyllis Gordon and their son Jack said yes. Jack was also hoping I could trade for some work. One of the first things I helped Jack with was the spring fencing. I also joined the weekend haying crew, but because of my work schedule I just paid for most of the milk.

Bob Gordon had just retired from Phinney Lumber Co.; he died the next winter. After supper on the nights we needed milk, I would go down after the milk while Nila put the kids to bed. Phyllis liked to watch the Red Sox baseball games on T.V. If there was a game on, I would set with Phyllis, and we would enjoy the game together. Jack grew up and remained on the family farm which was named "Findview Dairy Farm".

Jack and his wife Carol were living in a small trailer at the farm. They had just had their first child, a girl they named Jenney. They became good friends and over the years I held each of their four girls on my lap when they were born. Jack had a very good friend, Roger Mason, from Gorham High School. Roger was a very good trapper and had a trap line on the brook down behind the farm. I did some hunting with Jack and Roger on the farm and on land behind Phinney Lumber Co. Jack had a very large gun collection, old, and new, and in between. To get enough hay for his growing herd he hayed the fields of many neighbors. I stopped to see him one time when he was haying, a field of a friend on Files Road. There was a large rock pile in the field with a few trees around it. There was a big porcupine raising hell in the largest pine tree. Jack said, "It otto be shot." I said, "I could do it right now."

He said, "Well, get it done." I had my .22 revolver with me in my truck, I got it and I shot it. Boy was his friend some happy.

Jenny Gordon married Jeff Grant and they are now running the farm. They brought up three children there. Jenny has a 4-H group, and they show animals at the Cumberland Fair; they brought home their share of ribbons. Jeff works for the Gorham Public Works Department.

BLUE ROCK QUARRY, W.H. HINMAN CONSTRUCTION, AND BLUE ROCK INDUSTRIES

In 1967 I was working in the Payroll Department at Blue Rock Quarry. They were billing work between the seven companies: W.H. Hinman, Blue Rock Quarry, Northeast Paving, Economic

Laboratories, Cumberland Sand and Gravel, Leeds Dand and Gravel, and Sidney Sand and Gravel. What made it difficult was that there was a lot of employees that worked for more than one company in any given week.

Then I got a promotion to W.H. Hinman, Co.; I moved back one desk in the same office. I was working in Accounts Payable Department where I checked invoices from vendors with the purchase orders. Making sure everything checks out and charging the invoice to the proper job. Another facet of the job was filing the invoices away by vendor down cellar.

The I.R.S. had made some tax changes, so it was better to be one big company. As of January 1st, 1968, they incorporated everything together as Blue Rock Industries.

In the spring of 1969 in came a couple of slick looking young I.R.S. Agents. They wanted to do an audit and I was assigned the job of looking up invoices, timecards, payroll records, journals, etc. and then getting them, all put back into the right place.

After ten days of this I asked them, "What are you looking for. Just mistakes or a second set of books?" I voiced my opinion: that they might find a small mistake or two, but not enough to offset their salary. But if after all the work we did to keep one set of books, they thought there was another set of books, they were crazy.

They had a talk with my boss, the treasurer of the company and left. Ya, you know it, I didn't get any credit for doing a good job exposing their overkill.

Shortly thereafter I asked about another vacant job in the company and was turned down. Well, if you're not happy, why don't you look for another job? I guess I will, do you want me to work a two-week notice? No. So, I went job hunting.

Jack Thomas Gordon
1947 - 2020

GORHAM - Jack Thomas Gordon passed away peacefully Dec. 13, 2020 at Gosnell Memorial Hospice.

He was born on Jan. 25, 1947, son of Robert and Phyllis Morrell Gordon. He grew up and remained on the family dairy farm, Findview Farm.

There will be no celebration of life at this time. The family hopes to spread his ashes over the farm next summer as were his wishes.

To read a full obituary, express condolence and to participate in Jack's online tribute, please visit www.DolbyBlaisSegee.com.

Anyone interested in donating in Jack's honor can do so to the Alpha One Foundation at AlphaLorg or Scarborough Fish and Game 21 Fish and Game Lane Scarborough, ME 04074

Dolby Blais & Segee
Windham Chapel

Roger Mason "Trapper," 69

GORHAM - Roger Mason "Trapper," 69, of Gorham, died peacefully on Dec. 21, 2014, doing what he loved the most, working out back on the peninsula of his family land. He was the son of Philip and Helen Mason (deceased). He is survived by his wife of 34 years, Sandra Mason.

He loved to trap, hunt and teach his granddaughters to respect the way life used to be in Maine. His nickname was Trapper and he lived up to that. As well as being an avid collector, you could always find him playing cribbage with his friends and granddaughter, flea marketing with his wife and im-

TRIP TO WADEL'S IN PENNSYLVANIA

Nila and I had been talking about taking up the invitation from our friends, Clyde and Dorothy Wadel to come for a visit in Pennsylvania.

When my employment ended at Blue Rock Industries, I told Nila I wanted to go. She was worried about the money aspects when we would get back home. I told her not to worry; I'd get a new job when we got back. I got one on the first try and it lasted 13 years.

Our son Richard was born 9-23-1966; their son Brandon was born 5-9-67.

We had never traveled on a turnpike and never that far with two kids. The Pennsylvania Turnpike was an old cement surface; we made good time and had lots of fun.

Clyde & Dorothy
Hadel
Sept, 2004

When we went to get off the PA Pike, we had to go around the on-ramp which brought us back under the overpass; this got us disoriented. You were looking at a blank cement wall, no route numbers, no directional signs. It was go right or left, but how to keep from getting lost was the question. There was a police officer directing traffic, as it was rush hour go home traffic. I asked him which way was west; he just pointed and said, "Go!" I said, "I'm from Maine, I'm not moving until you tell me which way is west." "That way, Sir," he said. When we made the turn you could see the signs that had been hidden from sight. Had we made the wrong choice we would have been a month getting turned around. We had good directions from there on and made good time with ease.

Clyde was working on a Dairy Farm at the time, so we had a lot in common and I could help some. The wives had some catching up to do. Watching the four kids playing and getting to know each other.

On the way home, the 1957 Chevy started burning oil; we made it before it died.

THE MOTOR JOB

My sister Nancy's husband Raymond Reitze had just come home from Viet Nam. Ray came into Fort Lewis, Washington, in September of 1968. After his discharge Ray flew to Montana where Nancy met him. They stayed two weeks with friends in Baker, Montana. They lived for a while in an apartment in Westbrook, Maine. Ray's first job was with International Harvester at $2.50 an hour. They had a 1963 blue Ford pickup truck.

Ray left International Harvester to work with Stanley Hall, a Dairy Farmer and well-known cattle dealer.

Ray had worked in the motor pool in the service and offered to help me do a motor job on my car. We worked on it late summer and fall of 1969 using a clump of three maple trees in the back yard to pull the motor. We worked on it weekends in our open-air garage. Before we took the motor out, I went to Sears and Roebuck and bought a whole set of tools and a toolbox to put them in. I still have most of them today, 4-22-2022.

We borrowed a Torque Wrench, Ring Grove Cleaner, Ring Compressor, Ridge Reamer, and a Cylinder Hone from my father-in-law, Lesley Moulton.

We would do what we could in the time we had on the weekend. Ray would show me how to do something during the week along with my job hunting. We were working in my backyard in Sebago Lake Village.

Nila went into the hospital for a cist on her ovaries and they needed to do a hysterectomy. My mother helped with some of the babysitting; Nancy delivered her daughter Lenore Marie on November 22, 1969, all in the middle of getting the motor done. We had to wrap everything in plastic until the next available weekend.

Both Ray and I were surprised not to see rust, but it came out OK. We put it into a 1958 gray 4-door Chevy, a motorless car I got from Chet's Auto Sales.

RAY SMITH OF RAY'S GARAGE IN BUXTON 8-13-1931 TO 12-4-2021

He was referred to my mother and he took care of her cars for years. He and his wife Althea became good family friends and helped the family get good used cars.

Ray also let me store my "Ford Tractor and Big Tex Trailer" at his place when I had to be away.

November 2020 Keith Davidson and I jacked up and put two new corner posts in his large storage shed. We also took down a dead oak tree on the corner of their driveway and cleaned up a large pine tree the wind had blown down on their Saco River frontage.

THE WINTER OF 1969

We had a blizzard. Ray Reitze remembers a 14-foot snow drift in the road on Route #22 next to Carl Young's Chicken Farm across from the Buxton

Grange Hall. Nan said, 'We had to go out and play in a snowstorm!" After Viet Nam Ray wanted snow so bad, we went up to his folks and had to park and walk across the snow drift, walk another ¾ mile to his folks 'house. The State crews had to bring in a huge V-plow to break the drift open.

EUGENE AND "BUTCH" AND BETTY ANN (MOULTON) DROWN

Butch was in the Navy and was in Illinois. He then went to the Mediterranean Sea, and then to Florida. They had come back to Maine over the Holidays and had to be in Groton, Connecticut on January second, 1970. He had gone down and found an apartment in Bayonne, New Jersey. They needed a driver to follow them down with a load of furniture so, I drove for him. He rented an Econo Van which had the new balloon type tires, a little bit different to drive. We had it full, passenger seat folded down, and a rug extending from windshield to back door, with just enough room to see the side mirror by looking under it. We left two days before New Year's; most people were where they wanted to be, so traffic was light until we almost got down there. There was one turn off that is a very narrow one lane to the right and down a ramp and onto a highway going East. Butch almost went by it and turned without giving me much notice. If I lost sight of him, I was going to be good and lost. I followed him, but I was only inches from the guardrail. We unloaded his car, and they took me to the Newark Airport. Now a lot of people were flying North. They had doubled up

Earl Ray Smith
1931 - 2021

STANDISH — Earl Ray Smith, 90, of Standish, Maine, passed away on December 4, 2021, at his home. He was born on August 13, 1931, son of Guy M. and Bertha (Lajoie) Smith of Standish.

After graduating from Standish High School in 1950, Ray met and married his wife of 69 years, Althea Kendrick Smith. They had 5 children: Pamela Smith Poulin and husband Larry of Standish; Joyce Smith Durkin of Saco; Michael Smith of Buxton; Timothy Smith of Standish; and Patrick Smith, deceased.

Ray was drafted into the Army during the Korean War. After his discharge, he went to work for Hannaford Brothers driving tractor trailers until 1966. He then built and opened his own business, Ray's Garage, Auto Repair and Service, in Bar Mills, Maine. Ray retired in 1994, for health reasons. Today, the business is owned and operated by his son, Michael.

Ray was a member of The American Legion of Gorham, a member of The Masonic Blue Lodge of Buxton, a 32nd Degree Mason of Portland, a member of Kora Shriners of Lewiston, a Life Member of the Buxton Hollis Rod and Gun Club, a member of the Southern Maine Beagle Club, a member of 5 A.M. Augusta, a member of O.E.S. of Buxton.

He is survived by his wife, two daughters and two sons; nine grandchildren, seven great grandchildren, and one great great grandchild; and a sister, Jean Petrizzo; many nieces and nephews.

Ray was preceded in death by his son, Patrick; his mom and dad; two brothers, Phil and Gordon; two sisters, Barb and Iva.

Visitation will be on Thursday Dec. 9, from 2 - 3 PM, immediately followed by Masonic Honors and a service at 3 PM at the Chad E. Poitras Cremation and Funeral Service Chapel, 498 Long Plains Road (Rt. 22) in Buxton. A celebration of Life with Military Honors at Maplewood Cemetery in the spring. Online condolence messages can be submitted at the funeral home website, Poitras, www.mainefuneral.com.

In lieu of flowers, please donate to Saint Jude's Children's Hospital.

the flights by flying every half hour, and every other plane was a DC-10. You waited in line, and they filled a plane and off it went. I missed the jet flight by two people and waited a half hour and went by DC-10 to Boston. Boston to Portland was now after dark and you could see the lights all along the coast on the way up to South Portland. He must have been flying by sight; there was no long level decent; he turned the plane up sideways as I could look straight down the wing at the South Portland Oil Tanks. Then, a quick level off and he set her down on the tarmac. I was home for New Year's.

MOM BROOKS' COUPONS

Mom saved coupons. To see Mom's kitchen table with thousands of S.H. Green Stamps and Rawleigh Cigarette coupons. Nila, Annette, Richard, and I helping her count them, putting them in piles of 100 so she could redeem them.

Mom used to get kitchen or household items, and, or, to get birthday and Christmas gifts. The two companies published a book of items available with a list of the number of coupons required for each of them.

OUR DOG PAL

My Dad had been given a big German Shepard by a fellow worker that was about to retire. He also had lost his wife and was going into assisted living. The dog's name was Pal.

We had lots of fun with him, even if he was slowing down. We have a circular driveway and one day when I got home from work and stopped in the yard to check with Mom, expecting to have a request to make a store run, Pal had laid down at the end of the driveway.

As I was coming out onto the porch with a shopping list in my hand, another young man came down the street and swerved

his car into the edge of the driveway trying to hit Pal.

Pal had a habit of barking at kids on bicycles. I think maybe he had been plagued by kids before we got him, although he never chased or bit anyone.

There had been some kids of late (recently) that had been plaguing and taunting the dog when riding their bikes by the house after school. Was this one of them?

Well, I jumped into my car and chased that guy down the street, pointing for him to pull over. When he did not, I started forcing him off the roadway. When he stopped and I stopped, windows down, I told him, "Not to get out or I would clobber him." Then I told him, "That if I ever caught him trying to hit an animal again, I would kill him." Then, I left for the store before I could get myself into more trouble.

ANNETTE 5 YEARS OLD KINDERGARTEN SEPT 1970 GEORGE E. JACK ELEMENTARY SCHOOL

OUR FIRST RENTAL

In 1970 Nila had a good idea, when the little house next door came up for sale, she said we should buy it for an investment and to help control the neighborhood. It had a larger lot but was built on a crawl space instead of a cellar.

I went to the bank and with a recommendation from my boss John Messer was able to get the financing.

My first tenant worked for Cinbro Corp, and I met him at the garage at Standish corner where he was having his car repaired. He rented it on a handshake. He turned out to be the best tenant I ever had. He helped me with some outside repairs. He also got me a short piece of four-four round pipe, which we turned up on end to replace the rotten wooden drywell used to house the water line meter and shut off valve, to keep it from freezing.

Brother Ralph and his wife Sandy Brooks were my second tenants when they first came back from California.

MOVING GRANDPA MCKAY'S GARAGE

Grandpa McKay had built a one-car garage at their house at 174 Spring Street in Westbrook, Maine. It was a small lot with a vacant lot next door. No survey had been done. When the next-door lot sold and they wanted to build, the city made them get one done. It showed that the garage was two feet over the line. They had to take it down and the lot was not big enough to put it elsewhere.

I was told I could have it if I could get it moved. It needed a new roof, so I took it off, then I hauled it home to burn. I pulled the nails on the part over the door and let it down on the ground in one piece. Next, I pulled nails on each side of the back and let it down on the ground, this let me lower the sides outward with the one-foot corners of the doorway pointing up.

When Ray came with the truck, we moved the front top v-piece to one side, then he backed in between the side walls. We put the walls on with the corners pointing up, then the back wall with the v-piece on top and chained it down. When we got to Sebago Lake we unloaded it in reverse order, and we were ready to reassemble. Then I put on new tresses and put boards on the roof and new shingles.

MEMORIES FROM ANNETTE AND RICHARD

The places Mom (Nila) took them for adventures.

Down to Grand Ma Moulton's land on the Grant Road in Buxton to pick blueberries and the pole line by our house on the Standish-Gorham town line.

To the mall shopping.
To Kiwanis Beach to swim and picnic.

To the ocean looking for sand dollars and sea glass and seashells at Two Lights, Crescent Beach, Scarborough Beach, Fort Williams State Park. Harmons Beach on Sebago Lake to swim or Douglas Mt. Lookout for a view of Sebago Lake.

Helping Grandma Brooks each year in the gardens and helping with canning; pickles, corn, tomatoes, beans, carrots, and jellies.

Working with Grandpa Brooks getting in and stacking firewood and some with Dad at home.

THE LITTLE DEER

Nancy and I were going to our sisters,

Carol and Al Archambault's in Deery, N.H. to help finish a rec-room in the basement before a New Year's Party. Al worked at Honeywell Industries in Massachusetts, and overtime had slowed the project.

Going down though Sanford we came around a corner, I saw what looked like crows flying across the road in the distance and one went up and down. Now this road had been rebuilt and you could see for more than a mile. As we approached a place where they had cut down a hill and used it to fill in a low place, I'm thinking that it would have to have been something bigger to have been seen at that distance.

We came up on a deer in the road, a car had hit it and thrown it up over the roof and back down onto the road. The fawn she had been carrying had been dislodged. I stopped and got them over to the side of the road. No one would stop to help, no one was home at the next house to get to a telephone, no cell phone in those days.

So, I put both doe and fawn in the trunk and kept on going, in a short ways, we crossed the State line. When we got to Carol's, I had her get a lot of newspapers, I put down what she had on the cellar floor. Then brought in the doe and gutted her out, Al and I were putting his trash and the bloody stuff in the car for a dump run, as the cop who lived next door was getting home, a close call.

When we got home, I went to an undertaker friend and got some formaldehyde to fill the gallon jar I had put the fawn into. You could see its little feet and head; this I gave to the Bonny High School Science Department.

WORKING CUMBERLAND FAIR AND THE HARNESS HORSE RACES

I had met Larry Simpson when I joined the Jaycees. His folks Harold and Virginia Simpson owned and ran Simpson's Hamburger Restaurant on Route #1 in Scarborough, Maine.

Larry and his sister Nancy had a food tent at the Cumberland Fair. Later he was asked to run the concession stand for the horse racing for two weeks after the fair. He then asked me to run the coffee urn and keep things stocked up during the evening rush.

I would drive from W.A. Messer Co. to the fairgrounds , get things going with him and then have a burger and fries for supper. Clean up after the races and head home about midnight. I was very tired at the end of two weeks. One foggy night I missed the turn off Blackstrap Road onto Falmouth Road and went straight back to

Prides Corner in Westbrook before I realized where I was. So, the only way home was to go back by W.A. Messer Co. and home.

Another night my car lights went out and I had to follow Larry. One mile from home we were stopped by a County Sheriff. We told him how far we had come, and he followed us to the garage where I left it with a note. The next day I got a ride to work and back home and picked up the car and went to the fairgrounds. They thought they had fixed it, but it did it again part way home and I finished with no lights. I made it to the garage again undated and walked home from there. I did the Fair from 1970 to 1982.

AMWAY 1970 TO 1990

Richard and Marion Green signed us up to sell Amway products. We went to meetings at their home in Hollis and got products once a week. I had a route that I had every Friday night. At one time a distributor opened a warehouse in New Auburn for about three years. Then we had to go to Lisbon every Wednesday, most of the time the kids slept in the car while we made the trip. Then I got a used van which had been on lease to Standish Telephone Company, had it painted white and put Amway Decals on it. I had

Come join our world

DISTRIBUTORS OF AMWAY PRODUCTS

people follow me to make contact to get products.

AMWAY

Then for a while we had to get products direct from Michigan by mail which was very slow. Then the Green's had to drop out. We had to find a new sponsor. We had met Stella Doak from South Portland at the New Auburn Meetings. We looked her up and signed up under her. Then for years we went to her home in by the "Tank's Farm" in South Portland. She had lost her husband Hartson to a heart attack. In 1990 we all dropped out.

One of the things I remember was changing my route to see someone else and finding out that there had been a bad accident at the intersection I would have gone through at that time. Another time doing the same thing to stop to see one of Nila's classmates. She had a bottle of pills in hand with bad thoughts. We had a long talk which helped her over a problem.

RAY'S OLD MACK FLATBED TRUCK

Ray and Nancy bought land on the Rich Road in Harrison, Maine and started building in 1971. I was helping him haul lumber to Harrison and breaking down on the Bolster Mills Road and walking for help in the cold with snow on the road.

The next weekend, we worked to finish the back roof, boarding it in and putting shingles on it. Saturday night he and I went next door to sleep in our bed rolls in the haymow of the old barn there. I also remember getting a load of sawdust in Casco at the old Hancock Mill located by the cemetery and lake for Ray's horse Cindy and I think it was more than once.

HIGHLAND GROVE DANCE HALL

In 1971 Neil and Deloris Dow bought the Dancehall from Bud Elwell who had built it. In 1953 the roof collapsed and was rebuilt. The Dow's ran the dances there for over a dozen years with their daughter Michelle's help.

1972 RAY AND NANCY AND DAD

Ray and Nancy's second daughter April May Reitze was born on 5-4-1972. August 1972 Dad Brooks retired from S.D. Warren paper Co. The gardens got bigger and better. All the kids have had a good time growing up helping and learning from Grandpa.

DAD'S PHOTO

ANNETTE, 6 YRS OLD, 1ST GRADE, 1971; RICHARD, 5 YRS OLD, KINDERGARTEN

CAROL AND ALBERT ARCHAMBAULT RICHARD STEPS ON A NAIL

Carol and Al were building a house in Harrison on land they bought from Ray and Nan. Richard was five years old and playing with his sister and cousins. The foundation had not been backfilled and as always things are thrown in to be covered up later, including pieces of wood with nails in them. Trying to hide he was "in" there and stepped on a nail. They went to Doc Knight down the street, and he happened to be home. He cleaned it up and wrapped it with a piece of salt pork to draw the stuff out so it would heal, a very old remedy.

RALPH AND SANDY

Brother Ralph got back from Vietnam to California in 1966 and he married Sandy Scheibel. In 1967 when he got out of the service, he had bought a 1959 British Triumph T-R, British Racing Green. From 1967 to 1972 they lived in California. Then the move home to Maine with the Triumph towing a trailer. They were my second tenants in our little rent, while they built the garage with an apartment above, while he was driving for Dupont hauling explosives. They lived above the garage between 1973 and 1976 and built a house next door to the garageapartment building. In 1974 he had a 1967 orange Ford Mustang.

Annette and Cousin April Reitze

WORKING FRYBERG FAIR

1972 the third year working part-time for Larry Simpson I was asked to add the week of Fryberg Fair, but I could only work the two weekends, set up and take down. On the first Saturday when I got to Larry's he had two pickups loaded with a trailer loaded behind the old one. He lived on "Long Beach" on Sebago Lake, on the Standish-Sebago town line.

Larry said, "You follow me in the old pickup with the trailer." I asked, "What roads are we taking to get there?" He said, "We will go to Sebago, up Hog Fat Hill into Hiram." I told him, "I have never been that way, and I was concerned." He said, "You'll be O,K., just follow me." I held my breath going up Hog Fat Hill, once in Hiram I had driven up Route #113 to Fryberg and Route #5 to the Fair Grounds before and was getting used to the truck with trailer in tow. This was my first time setting up the tent and putting the equipment together. It was a chore, but Larry was a good teacher with patience, and all went well. Working the fair is some different then, being in the crowd.

The next weekend the take down went well, Larry had the routine down well, just wait for his lead and instructions. The trip home Hog Fat Hill was still on my mind, I went down that thing so slow as I knew you were still going down at the stop sign and you had to make a right-hand turn, I made it, what a relief.

SUMMER REC AT GEORGE E. JACK SCHOOL 1973 AND 1974

Nila signed up the kids, Annette 8, Richard 7. Their counselor Tom had them running track, swimming at Kiwanis Beach, Arts and Crafts, playground games, field trips, one to Gray Animal Farm.

W.A. MESSER COMPANY DEEP SEA FISHING TRIP JULY 1974

John Messer purposed to his father Jack the idea of a company picnic or outing when he came on board after finishing college. At the time the crew, office, and Parts Department were all men. They voted for a deep-sea fishing trip, it ended up a cruise just outside the Portland Harbor, fishing off the harbor floor by jigging. I had Ray Cole on my right and Joe Mullins on my left. We had a pool for the first fish, the biggest fish and the most fish. We all had the same kind of poles and jugs. Beginner's luck maybe, I won them all plus the joker or bobby prize. I caught the first fish which turned out to be the biggest fish and the most fish. Joe caught one fish less than I did, and the next to the biggest. Ray only caught a small octopus, and our side of the boat way out did the other side. Then I got the line on the reel messed up, so I let it all out and some of it lay on the bottom. When I reeled it in it was coming easy than a heavy jerk, as the line took up because the hook had caught into a mussel on a softball size rock, so up he came rock and all. I took a little ribbing, but so what I came home with the money, all of it.

1975 JOE THE LITTLE PONY

The neighbor of one of my Amway customers had a small pony for her grandchildren. His name was Joe, the name had stayed the same as he had moved from place to place. The kids were not taking proper care of him and were running his little legs up and down the tarred road as fast as he could go.

She was looking for a good home for him. I talked with Nila about it and then Annette and Richard to let them know that

argumentation when we had to find a new home for Joe in the fall. The pony had been given to her, all she had to do was to buy a saddle, and that was all she wanted to be reimbursed for. The kids mine and the neighbors, had a good summer. They learned some responsibilities for taking care of animals. Not to hurt them by mistreating them.

As fall was approaching,. I advertised that we had a very good-natured pony for a good home and $200.00 for the saddle. Which was just what I had paid for it.

A vet in Gorham had a Stallion for himself, a horse for his wife and wanted the pony for his daughter. He came with a horse trailer and wanted to give him a sedative, before loading him. I said it was not needed and led Joe into the trailer like he had done it every day of his life.

About two months later while they were out riding, a car spooked his horse which threw him off and he broke his neck and he died.

NAN AND RAY PUT A TRAILER AT MOM AND DAD'S 1975 TO 1980.

After selling the house in Harrison they moved back to Standish. As Dad had retired, he started riding with his son-inlaw Ray, helping what he could and being good company.

A note from Ray, *"Mr. and Mrs. Brooks and Me."*

I got to know Mr. and Mrs. Brooks better after Nancy and I got married. I know I was too shy in the beginning. One thing for certain that was always the same, I was always welcome, and they treated me very nice. They accepted and liked me just the way I was and when I asked either one a question, they always gave me an honest answer.

I loved Mrs. Brooks' sour pickles and baked beans, also Dandelion greens and her shell beans.

I remember going over and rebuilding the septic system with Mrs. Brooks, so I knew what she wanted. I got the permit from the plumbing inspector who lived about a mile up the road. I put in a new system as the old one had failed. I made sure the system would never back up again by running it into the old barn cellar.

I always felt Mrs. Brooks was clairvoyant and saw far more than people ever knew. Nancy helped at Prouts Neck cleaning houses and ironing Curtains.

I got to know Mr. Brooks really well after he retired and started helping me when I was digging wells and putting in water lines. He was a pleasure to have with me and I enjoyed his company. When we were digging the wells, he kept an eye on where the veins were coming in. He manned the ropes on the tile setting rig so no one ever had to go down in a well to make adjustment. He put cement on each tile before we hooked up the tile setting rig. When we were digging water lines, he would unroll the plastic water line, while I was digging the trench. He was a great help laying pipe and putting hay on the septic systems.

Mr. Brooks taught me how to fell trees when we were cutting wood. I knew how to run the chain saw but didn't know much about felling trees. He showed me where to make the cuts and where to put the wedges. I will forever remember his words, "Little Blows Kills the Devil Nip." He was soft spoken and direct on how hard I hit a wedge.

Whatever we were going to do, when he came over he would knock on our door to the trailer and would always say, "Good Morning Sunshine." To this day I can stop and hear his voice saying: "Good Morning Mr. Sunshine and Little Blows Kills the Devil Nip."

I was always greeted with open arms when I entered their home. To me Mr. and Mrs. Brooks were very special down to earth people.

Mr. and Mrs. Brooks have a special place in my heart. I truly hope God gave them Angle Wings, for they were special. I love you both and thank you for everything. Signed Ray, Sir Sunshine.

DAD'S BOSTON RED SOX'S GAME

For Father's Day in 1976 I took Dad and Mom to a Boston Red Sox's baseball game. We drove down to Haverhill Station outside of Methuen, Mass. and parked at a gas station that did parking on game days.

The" T" and extension of the subway system starts at street level and goes up on the elevated T-Bars until it crosses the Charles River and drops down and becomes part of the subway system.

We had just got elevated when we looked down and saw a woman walking on the sidewalk below us, all of a sudden, she squats down and pees. This shocked my mother, and she told, that story for some time.

We wondered how we would know which stop was near the ballpark. No problem, two-thirds of the passengers with T-shirts, hats, and ball gloves got up and exitedfollow the leader.

Attendants helped us find our seats in row 12 between third base and home plate. Dad enjoyed Fenway Park and we got to meet some of the players, and Catcher Carlton Fisk signed an autograph before the game, and they won. We talked about the game for weeks.

RICHARD IN WEEBALO'S – SCOUT MASTER MIKE DELCOURT

Richad says he remembers most of the BB Gun safety program, and Mike taking them to Dover-Foxcroft for a shoot off. He said he also had to make a cake for one of the meetings. 1976 and he was 9 years old and in the fourth grade.

JAYCEES SEEKING A CHANGE

Kenn Brooks chairman of a petition drive sponsored by the Standish Jaycees and presented it to the selectmen. Seeking a change in the number of selectmen from, three to five. We also wanted them to be open a few hours later one night a week.

The people who work a 40-hour week can't get to see a selectman. The second petition calls for the election of members of the planning board and the budget committee. At the time they were appointed by the selectmen.

The selectman's office hours are 8 a.m. to 5 p.m. on Thursdays. The Jaycees felt that the hours limited who could run for office as it ruled out those who worked a 40-hour week. At the polls, we lost by a small margin.

SEEKING CHANGE — Ken Brooks, left, presents petitions for changes in town government to Harold E. "Ned" Dolloff, Standish selectman. Brooks was unable to reach a selectman at the town office late Thursday afternoon and had to find Dolloff at his home on the Oak Hill Road here. One of the articles in the petitions seeks to make the selectmen more accessible to the citizenry.

LITTLE LEAGUE BASEBALL

Spring of 1976 I was Assistant Coach and Richard did not play much.

Spring of 1977: when I went to the first meeting to get the summer program going, Art Riley was the league director. He said that he needed two more coaches, one for a replacement and one to add another team. I said I would do one and see if the Jaycee's would sponsor it. They did and it was called the Jaycees. I did two years with Randy Dunton as assistant coach.

I had to learn a lot about coaching, but I enjoyed the kids so much. We finished in next to last place and improved it one notch the second year. But Randy and I made sure that each kid got playing time in at least every other game. On some teams the 9-year-olds did not play much,

which happened with Richard his first year.

Summer of 2022 Richard and I came up with this list of names from memory. Robert and Jeff Arsenault, Shawn Birdwood, Richard Brooks, Noel Brown, Randy Dunton Jr., Darren and Shawn Goulet, Jimmy Goodale, Patrick Healy, John Lavasser, Steve LaPierre, Bruce Lee, Chris and Scott Romma, Will and Mike Sanborn, Seth and Micha Sawyer, Dean Sawyer, Jr., Mike Simpson, Craig Thorne, Butch and Mike Tompsom,. David and Scott Weymouth, Brian and Jeff Wescott, Mark Whitman, Colby and Erik Yates. The score keeper was Annette Brooks.

WILLIAM AND FLORENCE LIBBY

About 1969 Donald and Sally Minor put their house up for sale so they could move back to Steep Falls Village and take care of his mother.

They sold to Bill and Florence Libby. They had three boys, the oldest one had married and lived in the Newhall section of Windham. The other two boys were coming and going over the next three years. The boys had a collection of seven old cars, no junk yards open, so they had a backhoe come and dig a big hole, crush them somewhat and buried them in the back yard.

Bill worked for L.C. Andrews Lumber and Building Supplies in South Windham. Florence grew up on Route #237 in Newhall.

The UFO, one evening while Bill and I were talking on my front lawn, we noticed a star size light traveling from one star to another, making a right angle turn and going to another star. We were looking West when it did it again and again and again. It went from West to Southwest, then straight up, then East and Northeast and then North and disappeared behind the North Star. Did it stay there or leave in the shadow of the North Star? We had turned some 300 degrees as we observed this phenomenon. We talked about this many times, and wondered how many moves it had made before we saw it and watched it?

Bill and Florence were very sickly over the years. Bill had high blood pressure and heart problems. Florence had Epilepsy and Sugar Diabetes and other problems. They gave her a pill on Monday to help one and by Wednesday one to fight the side effects of Monday's pill.

They were both taken by ambulance to the Maine Medical Center several times. Finally, the doctors told them they had to move closer to the hospital as they might not get there, next time.

Nila and I knew they were planning to move, and Nila also knew Bill and I were country music lovers and had heard about a coming event. The Doc. Williams country show with Smoky Bleacher were going to be in Portland. She suggested I take Bill and then got tickets. Bill and I had a great time. Smoky put on a skit about going to his first ice hockey game. His description of the players chasing and hitting that black piece of wood. I wish I had a copy of that discursive and funny ballad.

When they put the house on the market to buy a mobile home in the Hillcrest Mobile Home Park in Scarborough on Route #1, we bought their ranch house that was 24 x 24 with a 24 x 24 addition which had 4 bedrooms. It was July 1977 Annette was twelve and Richard was eleven and they were in Johnson Middle School. After we moved in, the neighborhood gave us a housewarming party with a lot of our Church party.

KEN AND NILA HOUSEWARMING

We sold our house to Ruth Moulton as a rental property and Nila and I managed it for her. Ruth grew up in Sebago Lake Village, had gone to Teacher's College and relocated to Anchorage, Alaska. At the time of the oil pipeline expansion, they were paying a bonus to get teachers. Ruth always thought she would come back home, but after retiring, she stayed there until her death. But being her rental agent led me to get into real estate a few years later.

SOCCER, TRACK AND CROSSCOUNTRY RUNNING

Fall of 1977 Richard was at Geo. E. Jack school and doing soccer with Mr. Robert Stack. He was a fast runner but not a good ball handler. Mr. Giberson the Athletic Director suggested that Rich switch to Track and Cross-Country Running.

HUNTING

That fall Richard started hunting with me and while learning hunter safety, and target shooting. We filled a jug with water and put it in the cove. Rich said, "I found out the 12 ga. Shotgun was no B.B. gun." He was literally following in my footsteps, waiting for the right time to ask questions. We were enjoying each other as we went through the woods and learning the area together. Trees, brooks, deer and animal paths, deer yards and the places were they bed down for the night or when hiding, usually on a high spot where they could see the opposing enemy coming with the possibility of an exit in all directions.

TOWN AND STATE ELECTIONS

Nila and I involved the kids helping in the distribution of flyer for the candidates in Town and State Elections and going to the town meetings in March. Teaching them why and how to take part in their community.

When I was the Dog Officer, I was doing two things: looking for stray dogs and letting the kids deliver flyers. They were chased by a German Sheppard, which I had to shoot to keep him from hurting them. Luckily, he lived after a visit to the vets.

1978 Little League Richard was 11 and Bruce Lee was my Asst. Coach and Annette was or scorekeeper.

1978 Track Mr. Giberson was A.D.; Richard switched from baseball to track and Mr. Bruce Dobkowski was the crosscountry coach.

HOWARD AND MARY RANGER

1978 Dog Officer onE my calls was from Howard and Mary Ranger who lived on the Bliss Road on the Saco River.

Howard called the Dog Officer for assistance after, "He had fired the shot that smelled 'round the world."

Having set a trap for an elusive porcupine with a heavy metal drag. Later they were aroused by a commotion outside the cabin. Mary said, "You've got your porcupine; go out and tend to him." Taking the old shotgun, he went out barefoot into the frosty moonlight. The roar of his shot danced off across the river and echoed all around. The night was simultaneously defiled by as dense and penetrating an odor as ever outraged the nostrils of man. Poor Howard! His porcupine turned out to be a large skunk with a twin brother that sprayed Howard. We rapped his body in an old shirt, jumped into the canoe and took it out into deep water and buried it at sea!!

Howard and Mary became good friends and Mary was an Amway Customer for many years.

There was another dog in Sebago Lake Village that was allowed to run loose. The kids would let it out. I was never able to catch it. I was glad when they moved away.

There was another dog much larger and older. I caught him at the end of Maple Street on the beach. He was good and friendly as I lead him back to the car, but when I lifted him off the ground to put him into the cage in the car, I must have hurt him because he bit my hand. I had to go to the doctor's before taking him to the dog pound.

Howard L Ranger
1935 - 2020

GORHAM - Howard L. Ranger, 84, died peacefully, Sunday, April 12, 2020, Easter morning, after a long battle with Parkinson's, in the presence of his daughters, Melanie and Maralee.

Howard graduated Deering High School in Portland, shy with white-blonde hair so white, he was given the name "Whitey" while working at SD Warren Paper Mill. It was that hair that made his late wife, Mary, fall in love with him as they met on the bleachers at Beech Ridge Speedway where he raced.

Howard and Mary married in 1958 and had a son, Clayton, and two daughters, Mel and Mara. He worked at the mill, developing a patent for a paper they manufactured. He would leave to start a flooring/carpentry business that ended a couple years later. He would become a long-haul truck driver, retiring at 73 years old.

Howard was a quiet man with a huge presence, always ready to help and lend his talents to anyone in need. He and Mary were active in their church, he was a song leader and Mary the pianist. He had a beautiful baritone voice and enjoyed singing gospel music.

Friends and family admired his strength, positivity and determination not to let Parkinson's diminish his spirit as it did his body; and, will be great missed by all who had the privilege to meet him.

Howard is survived by his two daughters, Melanie Ranger and Maralee Ranger. He was predeceased by his wife, Mary Aslin; and son, Clayton Ranger.

A memorial service will be held when given the OK by the state to congregate.

To express condolences and to participate in Howard's online tribute, please visit www.DolbyBlaisSegee.com

Dolby Blais & Segee
Windham Chapel

11-9-1978 REAPPOINTED DOG OFFICER THROUGH 3-10-1979

Date 11/9/78

By authority vested in us by law we, The Selectmen of Standish, Maine hereby appoint, or/ ~~grant~~ ~~a~~ ~~permit~~ to

Kenneth R. Brooks

as Dog Officer

for the Town of Standish. This (appointment or ~~permit~~)/expires Date March 10, 1979

Selectmen of
Standish

THE LOST DOG

I got a phone call from a salesman from Massachusetts as he had lost his hunting dog at Two Trails Restaurant in Standish, Maine. He was returning home after making sales calls and stopped for lunch. After lunch, when he got to the car, he let the dog out for a bathroom run. He said he never had a problem having him get back into the car, but this time, he took off after a female dog. He had to be back to his office for a sales meeting and could not go looking for him.

If I found him, would I keep him and not take him to the pound where he might pick up something from other animals. He said he would pay something for the service as it would be three days before he could come up to retrieve him and told me what kind of do0g food to get for him. I told him my son and I would do that for him.

The next morning someone that lived near the restaurant called. They had the dog and hoped I might have been called by the owner as they also did not want to see it go to the pound. I told them I had received a call from the owner and would keep it for him. On Saturday, there was a happy reunion. The dog was some happy to see his master and him likewise. He gave my son Richard a tip for helping Dad with dog sitting. When he got home, he wrote a nice letter to the selectmen.

THE DOG WAS SMARTER THAN THE OWNER

The owner let his Doberman run the neighborhood and people were a little leery and called me.

When I went to give the owner a warning, he got pretty uppity and was not going to listen and o0rdered me off his property.

I left and as I was going through Sebago

Lake Village, there was a Deputy Sheriff in his car at the local store. I stopped and introduced myself as he was new to me. He was filling in for the night. He stood six-foot tall and was a big man. He said, "Get in and we'll go see about this."

The owner was some surprised when we were back there in less than ten minutes. He was still a little belligerent and the officer said to him, "Do you want to go jail and have the dog put in the pound."

"Well, no," he said. The officer said, "I want you to think about this, to own a dog with a bad reputation, maybe not your dog, but the breed means you take on a duty to protect everyone else."

We left to let him think it over, he must have, we had no more problems on School Street.

KENN. RICHARD, ANNETTE, AND NILA

LINCOLN CLUB OF PORTLAND, MAINE

February 1979 after attending the Cumberland County Republican Committee meeting, I decided to join the Cumberland County Lincoln Club of Portland, Maine. To help candidates get elected by working in Standish on the get out to vote campaign.

1979 SUMMER BABE RUTH LEAGUE

Robert Sanborn was the Coach and I became the Asst. Coach. Richard was not in the top of the group and lost interest. He was not a good hitter and liked running better. That was our last year in baseball.

RUSS AND ROSE STOVER AND SON TROY

They had moved down from the North and started attending our church. Russ was an unforgettable "Mainah", and a very good carpenter. We had them over for a few Sunday dinners.

Russ did some repairs at the church and we were redoing our kitchen at the time and Russ would help for a couple of hours before getting Troy home to get him ready for school.

Russ had some old tools and used an adze to make boards look old as if hand hewn. We did the archway into the dining room and then stained it. Everyone liked it and wanted to know how it was done. When school was out, they moved back up North.

1979 summer rec Richard went to a meet at Scarborough High School track.

1979 the kids were in Johnson Jr. High. We went to several Maine Mariners hockey games at the Portland Civic Center.

1-16-1980 JOINED THE KIWANIS CLUB OF STANDISH, MAINE

Proposal for Membership

To the Board of Directors of the Kiwanis Club of

Standish

I take pride in proposing

Kenneth Richard Brooks

as an active member of the club and have confidence that he will become a valuable member.

1/16/80 — Paul B. Wats[...]
DATE — SIGNATURE OF PROPOSER
— SIGNATURE OF ENDORSER

PERSONAL INFORMATION

FULL NAME	Kenneth Richard Brooks	NICKNAME	Ken
HOME ADDRESS	RFD 2, Box 8	HOME PHONE	642-2756
CITY OR POST OFFICE	Sebago Lake,	STATE OR PROVINCE	Maine
		ZIP CODE	04075
BUSINESS OR FIRM NAME	W. A. Messer	POSITION HELD	Ass't to Office Manager
TYPE OF BUSINESS	Computers	DESCRIBE PRODUCT	
BUSINESS ADDRESS	Warren Avenue,	BUS. PHONE	854-9751
CITY OR POST OFFICE	Westbrook,	STATE OR PROVINCE	Maine
		ZIP CODE	04092

IF FORMER KIWANIAN PLEASE ENTER CLUB NAME, CITY, AND STATE OR PROVINCE.

NEW MEMBER ADD FORM
(ALSO USED FOR HONORARY AND NON-MEMBER SUBSCRIPTIONS TO THE KIWANIS MAGAZINE)

STANDISH

LAST NAME	FIRST NAME	INITIAL
Brooks	Kenneth	R

CITY	STATE OR PROVINCE	ZIP OR POSTAL CODE
Sebago Lake	Maine	04075

ENTRY DATE: 1/23/80

CLASS OF MEMBERSHIP
- ☒ ACTIVE
- ☐ HONORARY
- ☐ NON-MEMBER SUBSCRIPTION

UNITED STATES

	ME	01791	0181 17

RETAIN THIS COPY FOR YOUR RECORDS

Let us have faith that Right makes Might,
and in that Faith let us to the end dare to
do our duty as we understand it.

Abraham Lincoln (1809-1865)

THE LINCOLN CLUB
Portland, Maine

DEDICATED TO
MR. RAY LITTLEFIELD
FOR OUTSTANDING SERVICE AS TREASURER
OF THE LINCOLN CLUB

ABRAHAM LINCOLN
LAWYER   STATESMAN   PRESIDENT

IN COMMEMORATION OF
THE 171ST ANNIVERSARY OF HIS BIRTH
FEBRUARY 9TH

Annual Banquet

Ramada Inn
1230 Congress Street
Saturday, February 9, 1980

OFFICERS

Mr. Donald F. Dyer	President
Mr. Ralph H. Johnston	1st Vice President
Mrs. Charles Peter	2nd Vice President
Mr. Charles Cragin	3rd Vice President
Mrs. Howard C. Reiche	Treasurer
Mrs. Percy M. Wallace	Recording Secretary
Mr. Calvin Hamblin	Corresponding Secretary
Mrs. Gordon Davis	Financial Secretary

BANQUET COMMITTEE

Chairman	Mr. Donald F. Dyer
Guest Book	Mrs. Ray Littlefield
Head Table Arrangements	Mrs. Ruth Boyd
Publicity	Mrs. Howard C. Reiche
Membership	Mr. Ralph H. Johnston
Tickets	Mrs. Charles Peter
	Mrs. Donald Dyer
Decorations	Mrs. Donald F. Dyer
Hostess & Arrangements	Mrs. Cora L. Brown

Social Hour 6:00 P.M.   *Dinner 7:00 P.M.*

PROGRAM

Chairman	Mr. Donald F. Dyer
Invocation	Rev. Edward L. Fenderson
National Anthem	
Soloist	Miss Roxanne Petersen
Piano	Mr. Howard C. Reiche
Introduction of Head Table	
Guests & Remarks	Mr. Donald F. Dyer
Guest Speaker	Mr. Jerrold B. Speers State Treasurer
Benediction	Rev. Edward L. Fenderson
Grand March & Dancing	Burton Beats Orchestra

TEN GUIDELINES

You cannot bring about prosperity
  by discouraging thrift.

You cannot help small men
  by tearing down big men.

You cannot strengthen the weak
  by weakening the strong.

You cannot lift the wage earner
  by pulling down the wage payer.

You cannot help the poor man
  by destroying the rich.

You cannot keep out of trouble
  by spending more than your income.

You cannot further brotherhood
  by inciting class hatred.

You cannot establish security
  by using borrowed money.

You cannot build character and courage
  by taking away man's initiative
  and independence.

You cannot help people permanently
  by doing for them what they could
  and should do for themselves.

ABRAHAM LINCOLN

REPUBLICAN PRINCIPLES

I am a Republican because:

I believe the strength of our nation lies with the individual and that each person's dignity, freedom, ability and responsibility must be honored.

I believe in equal rights, equal justice and equal opportunity for all, regardless of race, creed, sex, age or disability.

I believe that free enterprise and the encouragement of individual initiative have brought this nation opportunity, economic growth and prosperity.

I believe government must practice fiscal responsibility and allow individuals to keep more of the money they earn.

I believe the proper role of government is to provide for the people only those critical functions that cannot be performed by individuals or private organizations and that the best government is that which governs least.

I believe the most effective, responsible and responsive government is government closest to the people.

I believe Americans must retain the principles that have made us strong while developing new and innovative ideas to meet the challenges of changing times.

I believe Americans value and should preserve our national strength and pride while working to extend peace, freedom and human rights throughout the world.

Finally, I believe the Republican Party is the best vehicle for translating these ideals into positive and successful principles of government.

DOG OFFICER – MY SISTER NANCY WAS LOOKING FOR A DOG

A lady had died and the son had her little dog and could not get along with it, keep it down cellar, not letting it out enough and it was peeing all over. He called up to see if I could find it a new home or have it put down. Jeffrey was a miniature Toy Manchester Poodle, black and brown. Nancy said she would try it and see how it worked out. Nancy said with a little loving care he did just fine. She and the two girls loved it and it was the best dog they had.

Nancy and Ray sold their trailer to brother Chester Brooks and bought a 100 A farm in Canaan, Maine.

CHESTER 1980 ERA

Prior to buying the trailer Chester had set up a target in front of a pine tree and shot right up the driveway. He was reloading shells and trying to find the best load of powder. All the shooting killed the tree. He lost enough hearing to keep him out of the service. One bullet made it through the woods, across the brook, and a field into Clarence Brown's barn a half mile away.

He had to have Raymond Reitze haul in two loads of sand to make a new backstop. Then when Leonard Stevens was working tower work, sleeping mornings, he would still be shooting.

From a youngster Chester worked to do his part, helping to control the over population of various wildlife, season by season, as he got older the game got bigger. The Wardens were always watching him.

Dad had been sick for about three months with liver cancer and we were taking care of him at home. I was lucky to be home and in the room at the house when he died on August 4, 1980. He was always willing to share the many stories of adventures through his life experiences and had a sharp memory for the details of his life.

MY GRAMPA

BY ANNETTE BROOKS A JUNIOR IN HIGH SCHOOL AT 16 MARCH 4, 1982

SHE RECEIVED A "B' ON THE REPORT I INCLUDE IT HERE

The person I am going to talk about is my grandpa, Ralph M. Brooks, Jr. He was born in Freedom, New Hampshire on March 30th, 1910. He lived on a large farm which encompassed over 100 acres

MY FATHER SITTING ON OUR FRONT PORCH

Ralph M. Brooks Jr.

STANDISH — Ralph M. Brooks Jr., 70, died Monday at his home here.

He was born in Freedom, N.H., son of Ralph M. Sr. and Hattie Stuart Brooks, and attended schools there.

Mr. Brooks was employed by the S.D. Warren Co. for 23 years, retiring in 1973.

He is survived by his wife, Lillian Black Brooks; three sons, Kenneth R., Ralph M. III and Chester L., all of Standish; two daughters, Carol A. Archambault of Harrison, and Nancy M. Reitze of Canaan; seven brothers, Amos D. and Miles, both of Center Conway, N.H., John D., Orion L. and Willard, all of Freedom, Robert W. of Kennebunkport, and Mathew of Interlachen, Fla.; four sisters, Blanche E. Brooks of Center Ossipee, N.H., Carrie Rowe of Dover, N.H., Lucy Works of Salem, Ohio, and Louise Moore of Conway, N.H.; and six grandchildren.

Funeral services will be held at 2 p.m. Thursday at the First Christian Church in Freedom, with burial in Lakeview Cemetery, Freedom.

THE AUTHOR SITTING AS HIS FATHER DID YEARS BEFORE

on both sides of the road as far as you could see and up the mountain on one side. It had numerous activities and chores going on all the time. He was raised to accept his responsibilities seriously. He was kind, caring, loving, understanding, reliable, and considerate. He had close family ties, and he went back to the homestead as often as possible. He loved the outdoors. He worked outside in the woods for many years. He worked with a team of horses that pulled the logs out of the woods. In the winter he used a scoot sled to put the logs on. Other duties he performed with the team of horses were hauling the maple sap to the sugar house where they made it into syrup, also after cutting the blocks ice from the lake and hauling it to the icehouse where it was stored for customers and for their own use. He was always on time. People used to say they could set their clocks by him. He never missed a day of work. He was married at the age of 30 to Lillian R. (Black) Brooks who was 18. They moved into a small cabin near the homestead.

Shortly after that they went to live in a logging camp where grampa worked. He could scale a log and tell how many board feet you could get out of a tree. Grampa knew all the different types of trees by looking at them.

Grandpa and Grammie wanted a place of their own to raise their family. Because they were tired of moving around every time Grampa changed jobs or the logging camp moved to a new location. Even though he loved the woods and working with the team of horses, he realized it was better for the children to go to school in one place. He wanted them to get a better education. Grampa wanted them to have *roots and a sense of belonging. He wanted them to have the feeling of being able to share friendships with people around them. He treasured the memories of his home and wanted his children to have the opportunity also. He knew education was extremely important. Grandpa worked instead of going on to high school and let his sister go because his parents couldn't afford to send them both. Grandpa's decision to let his sister go on to school did not enable him to get his high school diploma which held him back from getting a promotion at the mill where he worked.*

To help his eldest son prepare for college he asked a special request of his supervisor to allow his son to work during the summer vacation before graduation when the rules were generally different. In that way it allowed his son to save enough money to finance his first year in college.

Grandpa got up early every morning at 4 o'clock as he thought that the day was wasted if he got up any later. He usually had a full day's work done at noontime. He always made a habit of going to bed early. Even though company was there he would excuse himself and say jokingly "it's dark under the table, it's past my bedtime. Good night." This was his way of saying good night without explaining any further.

For a few years after I was born, we lived with my grandparents. This was an important time for my grandpa because I was his first grandchild. At night before grandpa went to bed, I unlaced grandpa's work boots and got his slippers for him. He loved to make his grandchildren happy. He bounced us on his knee and sang to us when we were little.

It gave him great pleasure to take us to get our Christmas tree. Grandpa and the rest of the family would walk down back through the snow in the woods every year. While we were all walking and looking at beautiful scenery Grandpa would be looking for the best tree according to its size so that when it was cut down not too much of the tree would be wasted. He would be looking to see what type of tree would last longer in the house. Usually, my dad used the axe to cut down the tree and Grandpa would yell "Timber" when the tree was falling down to the ground. Everyone would laugh. Then Dad and Grandpa would cut the boughs off the tree. My brother and I helped carry the boughs of the tree. Then when we were old enough, we helped carry the tree. The tree would be stood up by the outside of the house until we made room in the house for it. When we went inside, we would stand by the woodstove to get warm.

He took pleasure in the simple things in life. He enjoyed being able to work in the garden or the woodshed or going to talk to the neighbors. He was willing to give a helping hand when asked. He would not impose on other.

He would always have a happy greeting for us when we visited. He would say "Hi ya nip or Hishbuck," meaning hello, how are you, which would make us laugh. Every Saturday night he would look forward to the family coming over for baked bean supper and to visit or play 63, a favorite family card game.

After the meal on the holidays, everyone would sit around and listen to the stories about what happened to him over the years. He liked to tell about their experiences. They were interesting and fascinating to us children, particularly the way grandpa told them. Grandpa loved to see our expressions as he told the true stories of their past. One story that kept us on the edge of our seats was the time that they were living at a logging camp. There were no neighbors around for several miles. My grandparents had no transportation in or out except to walk or ride the workhorses. Grandpa had to work late, and grandma was in the camp with the baby. She expected grandpa home for supper at any time. She heard the icebox open and close outside near the door of the camp and thought it was grandpa. She started towards the door and her intuition told her not to open the door and she felt very strange. She wondered why he did not come in. Then she went to the other room and picked up the baby (my dad) and sat holding the baby on the edge of the bed for what seemed to be a very long time. Grandpa arrived an hour later and came into the house. Grammie said, "Why didn't you come in? What have you been doing out there?" Grandpa said, "What do you mean? I just got home." But he could not convince her that it was true.

The next morning when they got up to have breakfast they went outside to the icebox. There were bear tracks on the ground in front of the icebox. They followed them to a large empty bowl a short ways, from the camp. It had been full of boiled potatoes the night before. They saw the tracks of a very large bear. It had walked around the camp. Grandpa said, "Thank goodness you did not open the door, but how did you know not to." Grammie said, "She thought it was grandpa but got an awful feeling about opening the door."

Over the years and through all the experiences, my grandparents went *through together. His independent character and his strong will carried them through the hard times even to the end.*

My grandpa was not one to go to a doctor. He tolerated pain without a word of complaint. He tried to cover up how he really felt. He acted as kind and as pleasant as possible, in order to hide how he really felt. He did not want anyone to feel sorry for him. Being one of eighteen children, he faced may situations when he or someone else in the family should have had medical attention. Many times, there was not a doctor available. One such time when he was logging, he had an accident. His ax slipped and cut his foot. Rather than leave the job immediately he worked the rest of the day and walked about a mile to the camp. From the camp he was taken by horse and buggy to the nearest village, eighteen miles away. Then he was put in a car and taken ten more miles to a doctor. He had a severe cut through his boot and foot. The boot had to be cut away because his foot was so swollen.

He respected hospitals but didn't want to stay in them. If it was absolutely necessary for him to have an operation he would go or if it would cure what he had wrong with him.

In March two years ago, he faced the most difficult time of his life. A terminal illness, cancer was suspected. After many tests were performed, he had to wait several weeks for the results. He was forced to make a decision. The decision he made explains how much strength he had. After all the facts were known. No medical knowledge would change the fact that he was going to die. Anything the doctors did could only prolong his suffering. His decision was to stay home. He did everything in his daily routine as long as he could. He was glad that his family supported him in his decision. He stayed at home with his family for the remainder of his life. On August 4, 1980, he quietly left us.

I love you grandpa.   Annette

EVERGREEN VALLEY

9-1-1980 Nila and I bought Unit 121 at

Evergreen Valley Time share Owners Association. We were looking for a place to go as a family after the summer hassle for a week in the mountains. On the West side of Adams Mt. is North Conway, N.H. We would go hiking and a few times we would go up cross-country skiing. They also had a golf course where we tried to learn a little of the game and also played down at the Kezar greens.

I OVERSLEPT

How could I ever forget that first morning of hunting season when I overslept, rushed out of the house, drove to my hunting spot to win the race against sunrise. When I got out of the truck and couldn't believe what I discovered. I had forgotten to take my rifle and the lead poison (bullets). I just couldn't believe it!

Going home to retrieve them, why I was going to miss the prime hunting time, that first hour of daylight. I saw a deer on the way back going to my tree stand and missed it, but I knew it was there abouts around, and you know not far away! To say the very least, nothing was going right!

Suddenly, as my head was chaotically spinning on my neck, something incredibly wonderful happened. I cannot tell you how grateful I am that it did. I woke up! Hallelujah! I was dreaming. Blessed be! I drifted back to sleep, I did so with high hopes that I would have sweet dreams – not sweat dreams. Off to good hunting you all.

MY FIRST DEER FALL OF 1980

Back in the days of hunting with brother Chester, I had been hunting with a 30-30 Winchester Lever Action rifle with open sites. I was O.K. on paper targets but missing the deer in the woods. We figured out that I was not bringing the front site down into the back site and therefore I was over shooting.

I sold the 30-30 to my neighbor Dale Smith and purchased a 300 Savage lever action, like Dad's, and I had Chester put a scope on it. The scope made all the difference.

Chester was working third shift at Sylvania Electric Plant in Standish. The day before we made plans to hunt together. He had me go into the wood before daylight on the Little Ossipee Riverbank and sit across from the Game Reserve. He would come in after he got out of work at eight A.M.

At the time, Chester had been hunting with his classmate Dale Smith. Dale was waiting for Chester when he got home from work, hoping to hunt in another place. Chet said, "I can't leave Kenn up there alone, not knowing I'm not coming.

Let's go find him and then go to your hunting spot."

It was very dark when I parked, and I carried a flashlight to see my way down the long old logging road to the swale grass in the old riverbed. The river had changed course at some time many years ago. At this point there was a big old oak tree, where I had planned to hide the flashlight and wait for dawn.

I leaned the empty gun up against the tree, I had to pee, then hide the light under some leaves. I waited 15 to 30 minutes until I could see well enough to cross the wet area. I then could see where a porcupine had gridled a large pine tree next to the big oak tree and obviously was there abouts around, I loaded the rifle and stepped down into the wet grass.

Well, all this time a very large owl had been sitting on a limb some twenty feet up watching me. I don't know why he had

had waited until I stepped down to leave. But he scared the beejeepers out of me when he hopped off that limb and spread his wings, dropped down to my eye level before getting air enough to take flight. Dam it took a second or two before I knew if he was going or coming.

After I watched the owl disappear, it took five minutes to calm down. Then I proceeded to a huge pine tree on the riverbank and set down to watch and wait. Zoom, a miniature jet, at least it sounded like one, for it was a whistler duck which came around the river bend and put down on the water right in front of me. Two feet down and four feet out. The duck began paddling around, finally moving down river.

A short time later a doe and her fawn came down for their morning drink right across the river, on the game preserve. I watched them awhile before they walked off up the hill without detecting my presence.

I want to think it was some 90 minutes later that I heard a car door shut way up the road. Now I really started watching everywhere. Unknown to me Dale had met Chester at 8:30 A.M. when he got home from work, and that they were coming after me to go to a different place to hunt. Chet came in the way I had and Dale came down another tote road on the other side of me and then followed the riverbank downstream. In doing so, he sent a deer ahead of him and towards me.

All of a sudden, I could see antlers shining in the sunlight. Getting ready I took off the safety and waited until the deer stepped up to my level in full sight. I reminded myself to calm down, aim very carefully and squeeze the trigger, I told myself. It sounded like I broke the sound barrier.

Down he went! Then came the boys and a long drag out with a 4 pointer. After the trip to tag it, I went home and the boys went to hunt elsewhere.

1-1-2022, 36 years later I can still see all of this very vividly and will till I die.

.

Lightning Source UK Ltd.
Milton Keynes UK
UKHW022157090123
415068UK00015B/1776